"God's Got a Plan and YoU're It"

Increasing the Significance of Your Influence NOW

JAMES L. BLACK, SR.

Published by Devan Ministry Solutions
9900 Greenbelt Road, Suite 157
Lanham, MD 20706

For information regarding special discounts for bulk
purchases please contact Devan Ministry Solutions:
240-232-6105 or pastorjbsr@gmail.com

Additional copies of this and other books by James Black, Sr.
can be ordered online at *www.adventsource.org* and *amazon.com.*

Cover design by Lee Graphix PR & Design Group
Interior design by Alexandria Manderson

Second Edition 2015
Printed in the United States

ISBN 978-1-4507-4765-3

DEDICATED

To my late father, John D. Black – I thank God for allowing this man to be born. I will spend all of my life trying to be half the man he was. I miss him!

To my mother, Claretha Newton Black – There is a reason why everyone calls you "Mother." I am glad you are mine!

To my wife, Maxine "Max" – My once in a lifetime, and an Incredible Lady!

To my son, James Jr. – I see you as the most powerful young man walking the face of the earth. I am proud to call you Son.

To my daughter, Raquel – your gift of determination is inspiring.

To my daughter, Stefani – cancer did not defeat you, and God got the Glory.

To my daughter-in-law, Cherri – thank you for loving James, Jr

To my son-in-law, William – thank you for loving Raquel.

To my son-in-law, Joseph – thank you for loving Stefani.

To my grand-children, Elyse, Elyah, and James, III – you have all completely messed me up. I am addicted to seeing you every day!

To my siblings – thanks for spoiling your brother, I appreciate it.

To my mother-in-law, Frederica – for your love, prayers, encouragement, and being there for us.

PREFACE

As a child, I always admired people of influence, or those who I thought had influence. I also wondered how they got it. And for those who had, but lost influence, how they lost it. I definitely don't want to lose a good thing once I have obtained it. Because we live in the "now" generation, people don't want to delay until tomorrow what they can possess now.

During my 30-plus years as a community minister, I have met thousands of awesome people who have no clue that they ARE awesome. This could be because many of them have never been affirmed or complimented by family, church or society. They don't believe they are in God's plan, and they certainly don't believe they have any positive influence. They are often judged based on their outward appearance, socio-economic status, failures, or some other perceived weakness. Somehow God has given me a gift for seeing people for what they can be with His blessings upon their lives. I don't see a crack addict on the corner, I see a future leader in a church. I don't see someone who just filed for bankruptcy, but a future business owner. I don't see a student with a low grade point average; I see a future engineer. I don't see a discouraged teenager, but a future missionary at home or abroad. Every human being has the potential for great influence in God's plan.

If someone is not informed (or reminded) that God truly has a plan for their life, they could spend their entire time on earth as a stranger to everyone, including themselves. It is my prayer that this resource will help children, youth, and adults alike realize and understand that truly God has a plan, and truly they are "IT" in that plan.

Our world is hurting badly, in part because of people and policies that simply don't care. I'm not sure I will live long enough to see that change significantly. However, one thing I do know: if you give God a chance to refurbish the awesomeness in you, you can become a significant force for His cause, and make a difference in the lives of everyone around you. The nine "P's" in the plan provide counsel for how you can "do all things through Christ, who is your strength" (Phil. 4:13), as you become "IT" in God's plan with great influence.

Be Blessed with Influence
James L. Black, Sr.

CONTENTS

ACKNOWLEDGEMENT

Thanks to Maxine, James Jr. (Cheri, James III), Raquel (Will, Elyse & Elyah), and Stefani (Joseph) for their encouragement and patience during the long hours of writing. Thanks to the editorial team, Alexandria Manderson and Maxine Black for editing the manuscript, and Sharon Wright for her copyediting work, to William Lee of Lee Graphix PR & Design Group for designing the book cover, to Wimberly Wolfe of W2 Productions, and to Glen Robert Hnot for teaching me how to never forget where God found me.

To all the youth and young adults of the Southwest Region Conference (1991–2001) and the youth and young adults of the the Seventh-day Adventist Church.

To all my community youth, and youth of other church affiliations that have shared in my ministry. A special thanks to my young adult friends in Moscow, Russia who allowed me to pilot the principals of GGAPAYI.

INTRODUCTION

In the beginning, God was so deep into planning that even if His plan did not work, He had a backup plan.

God created man and gave him the choice to serve God or not to serve Him. Man would not be forced, but could choose of his own free will to serve and honor God out of love and respect. According to Genesis chapter 3, man failed the test, but God was prepared. You see, even before God created man, He had a rescue plan, just in case man would turn his back on his Creator.

If man sinned, he would face eternal death. So God offered His Son before creation to be the sacrifice--the rescue plan--that would bring man back to God. Jesus is the plan, "the lamb slain before the foundation of the world." (Rev. 13:8)

In connection with this plan is another plan, and it involves you. That's right! You're "IT" in the plan! You're the influence in God's plan to help save someone through Jesus Christ. You're part of God's "Plan A" for specific situations that may arise in your life. God is all about blessing His people, and He blesses people through people. God can and will use your influence in His plan to be a blessing to…

- Someone you know
- A stranger
- A family member
- A neighbor
- A classmate
- A co-worker

- A friend
- A best associate
- An enemy
- Yourself

Again, you're part of God's "Plan A" for specific situations. God needs you in His plan to be…

- His Instrument
- His Voice
- His Hands
- His Feet
- His Heart
- His Ears
- His Love
- His Vehicle
- His Destination in someone's life
- His Influence

"Here am I, Lord. Send me…" (Is. 6:8)

The following chapters will show you how to increase the significance of your influence NOW, and how to cooperate as the "It" in God's plan.

God's got a plan and yoU're it!

CHAPTER 1

PERSUADE YOURSELF OF THE PLAN

Let Every Man be Persuaded

Are you persuaded that you know the answers to the following questions:

- Who is for you?
- Who's got your back?
- Who is in your corner?
- Who is pushing you forward?
- Who is motivating you?
- Who truly believes you can do it?
- Who can you trust to tell you the truth?
- Who is actually praying for you?
- Who really wants you to succeed?
- Who wants you to be forever faithful?
- Who will recommend you?
- Who will support you?
- Who will pick you up if you fall?
- Who will be there for you, no matter what?

The truth of the matter is, although you have answers to many of these questions, you may not be really persuaded of some of the answers. Reality says there are people in your circle who want you to succeed--but not beyond them. There is something about human nature that cannot handle seeing what God can successfully accomplish through YOU. Sometimes people you thought you could trust will do every sneaky thing they can think of to sabotage or derail your success.

Nonetheless, I am so glad the rest of the chapter does not dwell on those negative possibilities. Rather, it's about the following questions:

- Are you for yourself?
- Do you have your own back?
- Are you in your own corner?
- Are you pushing yourself?
- Are you motivating yourself?
- Do you believe you can do it?
- Will you tell yourself the truth?
- Are you praying for yourself?
- Do you want you to succeed?
- Do you want to be forever faithful?
- Will you recommend yourself?
- Will you support yourself?
- Will you pick yourself up if you fall?
- Will you be there for yourself, no matter what?

These are not selfish questions. Instead, they are questions that should persuade us to see how God wants to use each of us. Romans 14:5 (KJV) says "…Let every man be fully persuaded in his own mind." God gives you the power to choose. Are YOU your own number one draft pick? Without question you should be! You are worth something to God, but you have to believe it first. You have to be fully convinced as you *Persuade yourself of the Plan.* God wants to increase the significance of your influence NOW, but you have to believe and want it.

Here is how God feels about you: "For I know the thoughts that I think toward you, says the LORD, thoughts of peace and not of evil, to give you a future and a hope." (Jeremiah 29:11, NKJV) If God has already planned my future, then I should be hopeful about what He can do in my future--and so should you. Being persuaded does not mean there won't be any obstacles, but it means you have a perception that can yield positive results if you embrace God's vision for you in His plan.

Persuaded by the Evidence

Imagine sitting on a jury, weighing the arguments and evidence of the prosecutor and the defense. Both sides think they can win, but they have to persuade the jury in order to get a favorable verdict. In your journey you will face the same thing. Your persuasion should be based on the evidence of what you believe God can do. Now that is called faith.

When Jesus chose His twelve disciples, I don't think they woke up that morning knowing that they were going to be chosen. However, they were all gifted in various ways, and Jesus knew what He needed to help bring salvation to mankind. Most of them were just ordinary men with minimal influence in their society. But being chosen by Jesus was about to change their lives forever. Although initially they did not fully comprehend what they were getting into, and they sometimes doubted, knowing who Jesus was, and the opportunities and possibilities ahead, made it exciting for them. They witnessed first-hand the power of God changing lives for eternity.

Though we still "walk by faith [and] not by sight" (2 Cor. 5:7), God has presented enough evidence in your life already to help you know for sure that He is real. Look at your foundation. What was life like for you as a child? What kind of home did you grow up in? Regardless of which side of the testimony you are on--the fact that you are alive, you woke up this morning, you are reading this book, you have some sense of direction--all this says you are a survivor for a purpose.

My wife Maxine and I got married during my senior year in college. Shortly after, we were hired as house parents in a group home for troubled teens called *Progress Place for Children*, in Huntsville, Alabama. This was an interesting, yet rewarding experience for us. I knew God would use us to impact the lives of young people, but I did not know how. Obviously there were very strict rules, and the orientation process was challenging. We worked hard to give our best to the teens who lived there. After a few weeks, I noticed that one boy named Tommy could not sleep. He would literally stay up all night and into the morning without an ounce of sleep. I asked him about this on several occasions; he said he just could not sleep. He was a big kid, and seemed able to handle himself pretty well.

One night as I was doing room check, Tommy asked me a question. He asked if my parents had ever tucked me in bed as a child. I told him they had, and I used to look forward to it every night. Then he laid this on me: he said he did not have caring parents. He had never once been tucked in before, so he asked me if I could do it. To me, tucking in means just pulling the covers over someone and making certain they are comfortable. I felt this was safely within the rules (it did not involve touching him), so I tucked him in, then prayed with him and said good night. I returned a few minutes later, and Tommy was out cold—sound asleep. I am amazed how the lack of love and the simple things in life can cause unhappiness in many people's lives. Tommy's experience was the evidence I needed to know that God had a plan for my life; truly I would live each day to make a difference. For the last 35 years now, my life has been about "tucking people in."

Persuaded by the Foundation

Parental Guidance: In our ever-changing society, the definition of family has caused much debate. While the arguing continues, the reality is that millions of children are growing up alone and "raising" themselves. Many of them are adrift, trying to create their own foundations. Foundation is critical to God's plan. Can you imagine a child standing on a corner panhandling, holding a sign that reads "Will work for parents," or "Will work for foundation"?

Foundation is a base. If it is solid, a skyscraper can be built on it. If it is weak, even a child could not stand on it before it sinks. Considering the broken families, juvenile delinquency, crime, poor academics, substance abuse, mental challenges--the list goes on--don't you wonder what kind of foundations are being laid in our society?

Foundation can also be compared to the "principal" that someone uses to begin investing money. In Matthew 6:21 we read, "For where your treasure is, there your heart will be also." We must invest in strengthening our foundations. Whether or not you got a good start in life, now is a great time to make a down payment--or reinvest in yourself. The good news is that thousands are making this decision daily, and are beating the odds. Make certain you are one of them. Let yourself become persuaded by your foundation for the good, increasing your influence.

Spiritual Awareness: Spiritual awareness plays a significant part in foundation. There is no question that I have a bias here, because I am a minister. We have to accept the fact that sin and evil has messed up everybody in some form or fashion. No one is exempt from the effects of sin. The Bible says in Romans 3:23, "For all have sinned and fall short of the glory of God."

For this reason, I choose to serve God and depend on Him for rescue. I am so thankful that church and family worship played a huge part in my growing up. This helped give me a decent foundation. I am concerned for children who are un-churched, who have no spiritual guidance to combat or balance out the challenges that life will serve them. They know nothing of the Bible or God's love for them. Prayer makes no sense to them, so they miss out on the daily privilege of talking to our awesome God and getting to know Him personally. If you have not experienced this yet, I challenge you to consider yielding yourself to the power of God. Allow Him to bless you spiritually and solidify your spiritual foundation.

Persuaded Not to Be Persuaded

It would be careless and naïve to think that positive self-talk can persuade someone that they can succeed, for real. Certainly many challenges will present themselves; you alone will have to decide how you will relate to them. You will be confronted with negative experiences in life that will definitely impact you. In essence, there are some things that should NOT persuade you--things that call for caution. One example is making excuses for the way things are. Many of us subscribe to compromise because of these excuses.

Family: Some feel that because they were raised in a dysfunctional family, they can't do anything positive for God and His kingdom. *Dad abused my mom and all of us kids. We lived in a poor neighborhood and there was not much structure. My parents divorced when I was a child, so I cannot have meaningful, healthy relationships. All my sisters and brothers are [you fill in the blank], and I am going to end up just like them.* I have heard it all. While we must be sympathetic to the pain caused by dysfunctional family units, please do not let these excuses persuade you that change is impossible. In these cases you have to be persuaded NOT to be persuaded. The cycle will change. The change can begin with you.

I was blessed to grow up in a wonderful family, although we had our issues as well. Both Dad and Mom were Christians who really loved the Lord. This helped lay a solid foundation for us, but did not stop nine children from getting away with things. I witnessed something at an early age that probably saved my life. We had a family member who was a chronic alcoholic. Everyone knew Cousin Joe. Every Friday, we'd spy him coming up the street towards our house in a drunken stupor and run to tell Mom. Because our mother loved him, she would place soft, thick quilts on the floor and allow him to sleep off the alcohol. Often he would sleep for two days straight.

One day as Joe was sleeping, I decided to see how knocked out he was. I stuck a broom straw up his nose and in his ears, but he did not flinch. I got down close and yelled in his ear to see if I could scare him awake, but to no avail. At that point, I was convinced of the dangers of any kind of alcohol. Cousin Joe's condition frightened me so badly that I could not be persuaded to join in social drinking at parties. Ultimately, he died from the effects of alcohol. I really miss him; when he was sober, he treated us kids nicely and was fun to be around.

Environment: While our environment is a part of our reality, we also have some say in whether or not it will negatively affect God's plan for our lives. Be persuaded NOT to be persuaded by the negative effects of a bad environment. Fortunately, there are many success stories of folks who grew up in deplorable conditions--but those conditions only motivated them to a higher level of achievement.

I met my wife in Brooklyn, New York in 1979. She was not only a young lady of beauty, but her manners and femininity were most impressive. She was the spitting image of her mother, who was an excellent model for her nine girls and three boys. I remember the first time I visited their Brooklyn neighborhood. I was a bit shocked, because it certainly was not one of the finer areas of east New York. I was impressed that no one in Maxine's family reflected the crime and poor conditions that surrounded them. Apparently, the Walker family was persuaded not to be persuaded by their environment.

Growing up in the Woodville area of west side Savannah, Georgia, we all had our little cliques and gangs. Deep down in my heart, I really did not like gangs--nor did I want to be a part of one. However, if a young teen did not have someone covering his back, life in those days could be rough.

I had a unique challenge in my 'hood. The fact is, I was not a good gang member, because I did not like hurting people. I remember when there was a race riot at my high school. Several White students were caught on the wrong side of the school property--some were hurt pretty badly. Because some of them were my classmates, I could not resist helping them. I even found myself apologizing for my African-American friends. On the other hand, my neighborhood friends couldn't figure out why I would do such a thing.

I had attended a Christian school during my junior high years, so the racial conflicts in public schools were new to me. I concluded that because of that sheltering I really had no "beef" with anybody. Did I understand racial tensions? Absolutely! However, it was not in me to be a bad person, to hurt someone because of the color of their skin, or because they were not from our side of town. For me this was reverse racism, and violence has never contributed to solving problems.

Ethnicity: People have experienced struggles between ethnic groups since Bible times. Something about the differences between people keeps our world in chaos. One tribe has to suppress a neighboring tribe; one clan or group will always fight another. Many have become paranoid because of the challenges of racism and tribalism. Racism is all around us; anyone who denies that is not living in the real world. So how do we overcome issues connected with our ethnicity? Do we have to share the same views with everyone else of our race? Do we allow others to bring us down just because we share an ethnicity? What do we do when their ideas are not in harmony with our spiritual convictions or values? (I will address this later on when I talk about my professional experience.)

The fact is, being persuaded by any issues regarding your race/ethnicity can limit your belief in God's plan for your life. Persuade yourself that you will make a difference for people of all sorts every time you are given an opportunity--and if necessary, create the opportunity yourself!

Persuaded by Perception

Are you easily persuaded by the perceptions of others? What is your perception of yourself? These are critical questions to answer as you attempt to understand God's plan for your life and determine the significance of your influence.

Personally, I don't spend a lot of time wondering how people perceive me, but I am concerned about being a positive example. At the end of the day, it's a challenge trying to please everyone. Regardless of what you do or don't do, it will not matter for some. You can make all the changes you want--standing on your head, flipping backwards, winning awards, even becoming a clown. Some people will lock onto a perception about you, and whether it is positive or negative, there is nothing you can do to change it. Therefore, don't live to please; live to be the best you can possibly be, and someone will appreciate it.

So, what is your perception of yourself? It is equally important to understand what is to be appreciated about yourself, and what needs improvement. In a 2005 article from *Psychology Today,* Carlin Flora states, "To navigate the social universe, you need to know what others think of you--although the clearest view depends on how you see yourself."

If you are seeking global influence, try some of these on for size. Do they describe the way you feel about yourself? Do others see you as…

- Spiritually connected
- Approachable
- Helpful/solution-oriented
- Respectful of others
- Balanced
- Healthy, with good values
- A positive influence
- A bridge-builder

- Someone with exceptional work ethnic
- Giving

Getting to the place where you think of yourself in these terms--and are confident that others do too--may involve some homework. But in the end you will find that acquiring these perceptions will allow you to better flow with significant influence in God's plan.

God's Got a Plan and YoU're It!!!

Increasing the significance of your influence NOW

Chapter One

My PRAYER:

Dear God,

I am persuaded and convinced that You plan to use me for great things NOW. Please give me the guidance I need to figure out how to use my influence in a significant way.

My PLAN:

From this day forward I will…

1.

2.

3.

4.

5.

6.

7.

Signature____

Date_________________________

CHAPTER 2

PRESENT YOURSELF IN THE PLAN

A Living Sacrifice (Romans 12:1)

Thousands of unemployed people wish they had work. I remember attending a job fair where one of the presenters emphasized: if you get a job, please **show up for that job.** Can you imagine an employer placing enough confidence in someone to hire them--then they don't bother to show up? If hired, you must present yourself; show up for the job.

Once you show up for work, many employers require you to clock in. Clocking in verifies your presence and provides a specific monetary reward for your time. Your work may be classified as full-time or part-time; a manager or supervisor will give you a schedule and you'll be told how many hours a week you are to work.

I can remember my first real job. I was the neighborhood paperboy. After a while I felt the need to move on to greater exploits, so at age 13 I got a job as a bagboy at the Piggly Wiggly grocery store in Garden City, GA. Wow! No other teen in my neighbor had a job like this. I was on top of the world. This was a newly-opened store, and first class service was required of all employees.

I remember the first day I clocked in. For me, seeing my name on the time card meant something. It sent a message: "You are now part of a team. You have a part to play in the success of this business. You represent this company." As a bagboy, I had a very important role. At that time, we actually loaded the groceries on a cart and carried them to the customers' cars. This meant that I would be the last store contact with the customer. My actions could determine whether or not that person returned to our store. Presenting myself as one who cared about customers, respected them, and appreciated their business was priceless to Piggly Wiggly.

As a result of presenting myself well, I was privileged to have job security during every college break. What a blessing! Each time I would return home, I would go to the store and be given a time card without question. Oftentimes there would be new employees who did not know me. But they would quickly find out that James Black had a special place in Piggly Wiggly operations! On several occasions I received tuition assistance from the company, in the hope that one day I would return and enter their management program. I was honored at their confidence in me, but God had a different plan. Still, the business perspectives I gained there will remain with me for life.

Before I leave this section, I have to admit to one crazy encounter that I was not proud of. In that situation, I took presenting myself in the plan too far. A shoplifter came into the store and stole some cigarettes. Once he was spotted, he took off running. Without a second thought, I gave chase. I caught him within a block of the store. I got the cigarettes back, released him, and told him never to return. Then I got in trouble for not bringing him back to face justice! Later, it dawned on me what I had done. What was I thinking, taking the situation into my own hands? Was I presenting myself as a sacrifice or representing stupidity? I will let you decide.

In my heart, I presented my all because I was "IT" for the company. Today, I present my all for God because I choose to be "IT" in His plan.

Present Your Gifts

The story of the widow's mite (Mark 12:41-44) gives us an example of what it means to present all that you have. As people passed by with their gifts, Jesus pointed out to His disciples a lady who did not have much, but gave all that she had. This is difficult for us to understand. How can someone give away EVERYTHING they have, even for a worthy cause? She must have been out of her mind. Yes, that is correct. She was completely out of her mind, and **into the mind of Jesus.** She had placed her trust in Jesus, and He did not disappoint her. She was a widow who may have been grieving still; Jesus brought comfort to her heart. Without that comfort, she might not have made it. The least she could do was show her appreciation for what our Lord meant to her. **To give all she had was the least she could do.** She doubtless regretted that she did not have more to give. Jesus said that her gift, though it was the smallest amount, was the greatest given.

A few years ago, my team and I organized a four-day convention for over 12,000 youth and young adults at the Dallas Convention Center in Dallas, Texas. This event was quite costly; we had to raise a lot of money for it to take place. It was a faith venture. I wanted to trust God and believe that He would come through for the youth, but I must confess that I had my doubts. As Seventh-day Adventist Christians, we honor the biblical Sabbath, which is the seventh day of the week (Gen. 2, Ex. 20:8-11). Well, Saturday morning was the peak day for the convention. The offering appeal would have to be perfect. Our goal was to raise $50,000. Special offering envelopes were provided, and we challenged everyone to give sacrificially.

At the end of the program, a lady with two small children came up to me and said they would like to present a special offering. The children gave me their envelopes; I thanked them and put the envelopes in my pocket. Later, I opened the envelopes and was stunned. The 6-year-old gave 4 cents and the 7-year-old gave 11 cents. I literally cried as I remembered them saying that they'd given all they had. I had no doubt that we would reach our goal, and we did. We collected over $55,000 because young people presented their gifts to God. The gift they gave was the gift they received. Those parents and children will always have a special place in my heart because of how they presented **themselves.** Their faithfulness challenged and increased my faith when I was not certain that God would come through. We can learn much from children's perspective of God, and their love for Him.

In Matthew 18:3 we read, "And he said: 'Truly I tell you, unless you change and become like little children, you will never enter the kingdom of heaven.'" (NIV) I am convinced that there are many children who truly want to do something great for God. Yes, God showed me that day that He could use children as the "IT" in His plan.

Now if children can present their gifts and talents, what about you? As you reflect back to your childhood days, perhaps you can see how you made a difference for God. Perhaps then you presented more of yourself to God than in recent years. The important thing is not so much what you used to do, but what you do NOW.

Present your gifts in the plan, because God's got a plan and you're "IT"!

Present Your Talents

I firmly believe that God has given everyone a special talent. There is something that you can do better than anyone else, because that is your gift. It may be a smile; certainly no one else can smile just like you. It may be your personality--no one is quite as nice and kind as you. Because you are "IT" in God's plan, you should always be mindful that there is something special that only you have. No one can compete with it, because no one can do it exactly like you. I am told that every singer or violinist has their own sound, and that makes what they have unique. Oh yes, many can play an instrument--but no one can play it just like you.

Presenting your talent as the "IT" in God's plan will only be a blessing if you use it. If you invest in it, it will develop and grow and increase your influence. But like anything else, you must nurture it for this purpose. Years ago when I was a youth minister in Texas, one of my responsibilities was directing a church camp for an entire region of churches. Horsemanship was a favorite activity. One of our neighbors near the camp raised thoroughbreds--some of the most beautiful horses you can find. One day she came over and expressed interest in donating one of her horses to our program. Needless to say, we were delighted and graciously accepted the gift.

The quality of this horse really took our program to another level. Though she was not the best riding horse for kids, her offspring became icons of beauty. During our youth rallies and parades in downtown Athens, Texas, everyone knew that we had a quality program because of these beautiful horses. Over the years we received many tempting offers, but to my knowledge we never sold any of those horses. Today the *Lone Star Camp* still maintains a top-notch horsemanship program.

Accepting that horse as a gift from our neighbor gave us the opportunity to see her operation close up. I could not resist asking if I could ride one of her racehorses. What do you know, permission was granted! One of the handlers brought out a beautiful, long-legged, athletic-looking horse. That horse had a natural attitude because he was born to run. The look in his eyes said, "I am ready to run, and ready to win." I finally found my courage and mounted. Before I knew it, he was off and running. I was overwhelmed by the speed. It was as if the horse had something to prove. For me, the message was loud and clear: "I am in the plan. I am gifted, I am talented, and I know it. I have been raised to run as fast as I can, and I seek only to win. My owners are depending on me."

Wouldn't it be encouraging if we had the same attitude? No limits, just take your talents and run like God is depending on you--because He is. The entire world is watching to see what you will do. You may not win every race for God, but you must still run. Run to serve those who need you most. Run to the homeless, the addicted, the fatherless, the sick, the poor, the discouraged--run to the rescue of anyone who needs you.

You are "IT" in God's plan. He is depending on you; accept His strength as you use your talents to win for others, just as He won the race for you. He is still running for you!

Present Your Influence

Everybody knows somebody who knows somebody. We live in a society where many are looking for a "hookup"(a referral or a recommendation). I remember working with several dozen young adults who had a passion for helping homeless people. We met one young man who seemed to be the advocate for addressing the needs of the homeless. He was well spoken, clean, focused, and well-informed about the issues. When asked where he'd learned all of this and why he was so passionate, he responded, "Because I AM homeless." Even the homeless have influence. He was determined to use his influence to be "IT" for the needs of the homeless in St. Louis, Missouri.

Presenting your influence in God's plan does not take much. You just do it. You never know who is watching you. You never know who may be impressed with you. You never know who you may be mentoring. God can use your influence to make someone's life better. This is why it is crucial that we "let [our] light so shine…that [others] may see." (Matt. 5:16) Be determined to use your influence for more than personal gain. Use it for the good of others.

When my son James Jr. was a teenager, he wanted to dress like all the other teenagers at the time--pants hanging off his butt, shirt un-tucked, sneakers untied, etc. One day he went to a job interview dressed like that. Before he got out of the car, I told him he was not going to get the job. He said, "Watch me!" I smiled and nodded. Thirty minutes later, he returned to the car with a dejected look on his face. I simply said, "Better luck next time." Later, he asked how I knew he hadn't gotten the job. I told him that his manner of dress sent a message to management that he was not serious about working for their company.

The following day we talked about the concept of dressing for success. We went to K & G Men's Store and I helped him pick out several suits: French cuffed shirts, cuff links, new shoes and the works. We had the shirts heavily starched and the suits steam cleaned. The very next interview, he was hired by what was then known as Nations Bank (now Bank of America). Afterward, he told me that the bank manager complimented him on his dress: how sharp and clean he looked, how rare it was to see a teenager dressed for success like that. The fact is, James Jr. walked into that interview looking like a person of influence. That gave him the edge for the position. Because of the fatherly influence I carried at the time, I made certain that he used his impressive new salary to reimburse me for the K & G clothing bill--with interest!

My son's plan to "dress for success" started a new trend among his peers. It was obvious, because going to church became a real fashion show; parents were pleased. The fact of the matter is that those kids liked what they saw in the mirror when they dressed up, and it became a way of life.

Influence can be powerful. Use it wisely. Do not abuse it and make things difficult for others. People with influence are often trusted, so be honest with your influence. Do not compromise what you worked so hard to get. Distinguish yourself from others without apology.

God's got a plan, and your influence is "IT."

Present Your Sacrifice – *No limits – Grace has no boundaries*

We talked earlier about presenting your gifts like the widow's mite. God has a plan for you that requires sacrifice. For me, sacrifice means all or nothing. How many of us are truly willing to lay it all on the line? Sacrifice does not mean depending on reserves. People aren't used to having someone sacrifice for them. "I'll be there for you," but sacrifice everything? I am not sure about that. You mean I have to totally commit myself to God's plan for the good of others? You may ask, "Why should I do that? What have they done for me?" Well, since you asked, others brought you into this world. Others fed and clothed you. Others provided jobs for your family members so they could survive and be educated. Others introduced your family to Christ, and because of that you have a decent life with purpose.

Working with prison ministry has been a lesson in sacrifice for me. I have met individuals who have made terrible mistakes in life, and are just looking for another chance. Getting involved with inmates and their families can be a handful. Often churches want minister to these individuals, but do not understand the depth of the problems. When the heat turns up and they realize the level of commitment required to make a difference, they bail out. Sacrifice means this is an opportunity: though it may prove complicated, we're with you until the end.

Many years ago, I learned a valuable lesson while serving as a student missionary in Port-au-Prince, Haiti. For one solid year, I observed how parents who lived in poverty sacrificed so that their children could eat. Many times they would only have enough food for one person--but they had to share it with a family of six or seven. The parents would go hungry in order for the children to eat. If our group of missionaries went to the park or the beach for a picnic, little children would gather around and watch us eat. It was one of the most heartbreaking experience I have ever had. Every bite of your sandwich was carefully studied by dozens of hungry eyes. Needless to say, we gave away more than we ate. In those cases, I found it was a great joy to give sacrificially. No doubt we gained significant influence with those children, because it was obvious that we cared.

Jesus serves as our example. In Luke 18:18-23, a rich young ruler wanted eternal life, so he asked Jesus about it. He was used to negotiating for what he wanted; he thought this would be a piece of cake. When Jesus spoke about keeping the commandments, the young man got excited. After all, he'd been a great commandment keeper since he was a child. But Jesus said he was missing one thing. He told the man to sell everything and give to the poor--then come take up the cross and follow Him.

Here was the problem: this guy had never had to sacrifice anything before. Jesus wanted him to understand that nothing he had could be carried on the journey to help others. First Jesus asked him to sell his *stuff,* then give the proceeds to the poor so they could get what was important and necessary for their basic living. In addition, for the man to sell *all he had,* it would include the clothes on his back. This would leave him naked. He could not see himself going from having everything, to being naked. Obviously, he was not ready to carry a cross for others. He was not ready for eternal life.

In essence, Jesus asked the man to do what He had already done. He came to present Himself as a sacrifice for all. He left everything in heaven, came to earth with nothing. Jesus gave all He had for others, even to the point of nakedness on a cross, and ultimately gave up His life so we could live.

The greatest sacrifice we can make is dying to self. We live in a "me-first" generation. People are programmed to put themselves first. Many race to the front of the line. There was a time when gentlemen opened doors for the ladies, but that's rare now. Not many people say, "Excuse me" anymore. The fact is, dying to self is an attitude. It means killing the spirit that prevents me from sacrificing myself for the good of others.

God's got a plan and you're "IT," a sacrifice for others. Present yourself today.

God's Got a Plan and YoU're It!!!

Increasing the significance of your influence NOW

Chapter Two

My PRAYER:

Dear God,

I present myself, my gifts, my talents, my influence, and myself as a sacrifice in your plan NOW. Please give me the guidance I need to know your will.

My PLAN:

From this day forward I will…

1.

2.

3.

4.

5.

7.

Signature____

Date____________________________

CHAPTER 3

PURPOSE GUIDED THROUGH THE PLAN

He will direct your path

There has been much discussion among some Christians about being "*Purpose-Driven.*" As a visiting lecturer at a university in Michigan, I overheard a group of seminarians debating the subject. The discussion was intense, and I would have rewarded both sides for their passion.

Following the discussion, I pondered the issue from a biblical and practical point of view. Proverbs 3:5, 6 provides the context: "Trust in the Lord with all your heart and lean not unto your own understanding; In all your ways acknowledge Him, and He shall direct your paths." (KJV) This passage has been a favorite and true blessing for me since I accepted Christ as my personal Savior and Lord. I am encouraged not to lean on my own understanding of God's plan, because my heart's commitment and my intellectual understanding may be insufficient for carrying it out. In addition, my way simply may not be His way.

Oftentimes, a particular destination can be reached through a variety of paths. But what is the most dependable route? I remember when I purchased my first GPS. I made the mistake of thinking it was an absolute, it could make no mistakes. I later learned that some systems did not include recently developed highways and neighborhoods. For this reason, I needed more than the GPS. I needed basic directions.

Jesus says, "I know my sheep, when they hear my voice they follow me." (John 10:27) For this reason, I choose to be purpose-guided in God's plan. Yes, I should wake up every day with purpose, but my purpose is purposeLESS if it is not guided by His purpose.

I have seen cattle driven in Texas and Montana, and I have seen sheep guided in New Zealand.

With the cattle, the cowboys range around behind them cracking a whip. But the sheep follow their shepherd.

It's admirable to be purpose-driven, but your progress is limited if you are not purpose-guided by God's plan to save. I have had thousands of young people ask me about their purpose in life. I have heard everything under the sun. Many are aware of their purpose, and know what gets them out of bed every day. Some have been dreaming for years about careers, life partners, and destiny. Now they seek focus and a plan to fulfill their purpose. I always encourage them to trust God, not themselves. I usually use my own experience as an example: I've made many mistakes because I knew what I wanted to accomplish, but wasn't always certain how to get there.

When I was in high school, I told everyone I wanted to be a dentist. I did not have any mentors in dentistry, nor was the experience of going to my dentist particularly pleasant. I just thought it was a noble profession and I could make a lot of money doing it. I was driven by the idea of wealth and the title of "Doctor," but I couldn't care less about healthy gums and clean teeth. I dreamed about the type of home I'd build, and the many cars I would own--selfish thoughts that would benefit no one else but "Doctor Me." This is my personal example of being purpose-driven without guidance.

As my journey continues, spiritual focus and faith determination are two key elements that have made the difference. Purpose-guided purpose is a definite. God desires that I am purpose-guided through His plan.

Directions: There is something comforting about knowing exactly where you are going. Some years back, I pastored two churches in the Texas panhandle. The churches were 120 miles apart and I had to make the journey at least twice a week for four years. The directions were simple. If am leaving Amarillo heading to Lubbock, I just take Interstate 27 south. One day I was driving to Lubbock. About halfway there, on the same highway I drove twice a week, I got completely lost. It was as if I had a mental lapse. I asked myself, "Where am I going, and why am I on this highway?" It was a very frightening moment. Then reality returned, and I realized I needed to go back home and get some much-needed rest!

We should encourage each other, and especially our youth, to press forward with purpose-guided direction. I am used to speaking with young people who think they know everything. You may be one yourself, or know someone like this. This is the person whose middle name is "Google Search." This attitude can be costly. If you are a leader, the price is even higher, because you are in a position where people have to follow you. You may be in student government, or a level 5 executive. Without guidance and direction, it is only a matter of time before you face a possible dead end.

In the mid 1990's, my family and I were traveling through Mississippi on our way back to Dallas when traffic came to a complete standstill. Apparently, there was a collision between two 18-wheelers on a narrow bridge, and no one was going anywhere for a while. One driver thought he knew a way around, so everyone began to follow him. Soon a long line of cars wove its way through a residential neighborhood. An elderly gentleman stood on a corner trying to stop the caravan, but no one was interested in what he had to say. As the traffic came to a complete stop, I rolled down my window. He approached and asked if we were aware that there was a dead end ahead. He quickly described the correct route, and we became the lead car that eventually got around the accident.

That man didn't look as if he knew much, but he did know that we were headed in the wrong direction!

Even with great purpose-guided directions, God's plan may include unexpected detours. Never lose your cool because of them. A detour does not mean your trip is over. It just means you have to go a different route. Your destination will always remain the same, but how you get there is up to God. Trust him--He knows the way. Often detours are caused by construction or a need for road repairs. Whatever the reason, construction makes the roads better for future travel. Purpose-guided directions will lead you where God has a plan, and you're "IT."

Knowledge and Understanding: When I was in high school, one of my teachers told the class that knowledge is power and power is knowledge. I have always been cautious with my beliefs; I don't believe something just because it sounds profound. Certainly knowledge is key in succeeding at many things in life. One must always understand the "how-to" in life. There are two kinds of people when it comes to purpose-guided knowledge and understanding. One group says, "I don't need a manual!" The second asks, "Where is the manual?" A manual does not just tell you how to assemble a product. It also provides pertinent information on operation and maintenance. Sometimes the manual can provide knowledge and understanding well outside of normal common sense.

Now back to the scripture I mentioned earlier, Proverbs 3:5: "Lean not on your own understanding."

While there is nothing wrong with my understanding, I must trust in God's plan for my life. The scripture is not insulting our intelligence by telling us not to depend on our understanding. Instead, it is making us wiser by telling us to depend on the One who is responsible for the plan. I may only know about sections A-D of the plan, but the Master of the Universe is all-knowing--that's A-Z and beyond! It is wise to depend on His experience. This characteristic of God is called "omniscience." He knows what was before the beginning, and He knows what comes after the end. I don't know about you, but I want to put my trust in that kind of understanding. He is the best advisor anyone can ever have. The newspaper horoscope will always fall short, but an all-knowing God will never lead you wrong in the plan.

On this basis, bring everything you know about the plan to Him. He will purpose-guide you through the plan. Remember you are "IT" in the plan. God's people should be well equipped with education and knowledge. Therefore, you should read and study and seek ways to cultivate your mind. You want to be careful what you feed your mind; it is the reservoir where God stores all the good stuff He's planning for your benefit.

The apostle Peter says we should be able to give a reason for the hope that is within us. (1 Pet. 3:15) This comes through our knowledge of Christ and our experience with Him. It is not meant to be one-sided. Those in God's plan should be well balanced with knowledge and reality. It does not hurt to have a little knowledge of many things. I am not suggesting that you try illegal drugs so as to have first-hand knowledge their effects on the body, nor am I suggesting the same with alcohol (i.e. social drinking). Rather, because you're "IT" in God's plan for drug addicts and alcoholics, you need a basis for offering empathy, understanding, and hope. If someone is in debt, you can be a blessing to them with knowledge about debt-free living. Being a well-rounded person significantly increases your influence in God's plan.

A wide knowledge base can also save you from embarrassment. Once I was traveling with a youth group on a mission trip to Kenya. We were at the airport in Nairobi on our way home, when I made a big mistake out of ignorance. There was an extremely long line for check-in and people were getting impatient. All of a sudden, a British lady walked around the line, directly to the counter to check in. Of course I was not going to stand for that! I am an outspoken American. I marched up to the counter and informed the agent that she had cut ahead of everyone. The lady was shocked, and we argued back and forth about what she had done. Then the agent said, "Sir, she did not cut the line. Read the sign above." The sign said "Advance Check-in." Those who had checked in online or ahead of time could go directly to the counter. I wanted to do a disappearing act. I was so embarrassed that the entire youth group had witnessed the whole episode!

I tucked my tail and got back in line. Because I was not as knowledgeable as I should have been, I caused someone else public embarrassment. After we checked in, I went to the lady and apologized. To her surprise, I asked her to forgive me. I told her that I'd witnessed several incidents where foreigners were very disrespectful to the African people. At first glance, I thought that was what had happened. She was moved by my willingness to offer an apology. Now I make certain that I pay attention to all signs!

Young people, your own library is an important tool that helps you to become current and knowledgeable. Begin building it up as soon as possible, whether in hard-copy or digital format. Start learning about places, travel, cultures, history, arts, etc. The information is there, 24-7-365. A digital library can be a convenient reference for you to find anything you need to help on your journey in preparation for God's plan.

Intentions and Efforts: Good intentions do not guarantee positive results! Thousands of youth travel on short-term mission trips because they think--or have been told--that it is the right thing to do. Many people in third-world countries look forward to these young missionaries coming to serve, because their need is so great. As a result, thousands of churches, schools and hospitals have been built. Can you imagine how many people are served through these efforts? We should applaud the leaders who organize these mission endeavors that give youth opportunities to learn how to serve abroad.

However, one thing may be missing. With all our noble intentions, we often fall short of the mission at home in North America. Perhaps our foreign mission endeavors would be even more effective if practice began right here. There is nothing wrong with sponsoring and organizing mission projects abroad. But because of our unique challenges, we are now at a point where we are seeking missionaries to come to North America.

Purpose-guided intention suggests that we should take care of those we see every day first, then branch out to other places. I was invited to speak at a large church that was celebrating the return of their youth group from a short-term mission trip. During the potluck after church, I sat at the table with several of the participants. I heard some heart-moving testimonies about how God had blessed the group. At the end of the day, I asked one young man what the group did locally in the community. He did not understand what I was talking about. I had to explain that I meant community outreach in his city. He said, "Oh, we don't do anything around here." I said, "Excuse me?" He repeated that his church doesn't do anything for the homeless or the needy in their city. This was shocking to me. While overseas outreach is good, I am not sure we are teaching the importance of taking care of business at home first. Like education and good health, hospitality should always begin at home.

God is preparing you to make a difference where you are. He wants you to be a regular participant in your local community. The homeless and the disenfranchised should know you by name. I have walked the streets with young people who found it fascinating that those folks have names, that they dream of the day when they might have a home. They met "ladies of the street" who did not really want to be on the street. They talked with other youth who were seeking a better alternative. They saw how they could truly make a difference. The best part is that it did not cost $3,000 apiece, and they could have weekly or even daily follow up with their new friends.

My intentions were good when I first started helping individuals released from prison. I had a burden for helping them transition back into society. I had a plan, but did not follow it. Soon my efforts began to backfire and hurt those I was trying to help. I realized quickly that you have to teach basic skills in order for many of them to be able to manage by themselves. For example, an individual may work and earn enough to live on. But what will keep them from wasting that money on drugs, alcohol, gambling, prostitution or other forms of mismanagement? Baby steps are needed first for those we intend to help, or our best efforts can hurt them even more.

Ask God to guide you in His plan to make a difference in someone's life. He will make certain you have everything needed to use your influence and effort in a safe and reasonable manner.

Compassion: God's plan for you would not be complete without purpose-guided compassion. Some have argued that the church has to be careful not to go overboard in this area. I don't know about you, but there have been times in my life when I truly needed overboard compassion! Truth be told, our world is hurting because people are hurting. I may not be able to save the world, but I can do my part. Perhaps we have become desensitized to the gravity of the issues around us.

In 1976, I left Savannah, Georgia, to attend Oakwood University in Huntsville, Alabama. I knew I was going to make a difference, though I did not know exactly how it was going to happen. While attending Oakwood, I participated in community outreach every weekend. There was something special about going into oppressed neighborhoods as a college student, being a mentor and just loving people. Perhaps it was easier for me to relate to people in these situations because they were similar to the neighborhood I had left in Savannah.

This went on for a few years, but then I realized that God was calling me to something else. I did not know what it was, but I knew that every time I watched one of those *Save the Children* programs, I'd be in tears and my heart would be torn open anew. I used to wonder what goes on in a mother's mind, watching her child starve or die from a treatable disease, and being unable to do anything about it. The United Nations Food and Agriculture Organization estimates that nearly 870 million of the 7.1 billion people in the world--that's one out of every eight--suffered from chronic undernourishment in 2010-2012. Almost all the hungry people, 852 million, live in developing countries. This represents 15 percent of the population in those countries. There are 16 million undernourished people in developed countries (FAO 2012; http://www.worldhunger.org). These are some mind-boggling numbers.

Even back then, I believed that if every person who could afford to give something would have a little compassion, we could make a difference. I knew that somehow I had to do my part, as an individual who cared.

In 1979, I took a year out of college to go to Port-au-Prince, Haiti as a student missionary. You can read my entire experience in my book, *God's Got a Plan and I'm In It!* That incredible year filled my life with so much joy, trying to make a difference by helping others. I had never been to a third world country before, and my first few days were nothing short of culture shock. I cried every day. I just could not believe that people could be so poor. Seeing it on television was one thing, but touching it was another. I quickly realized that I had work to do, and I must get busy. The Haitian people influenced my life for eternity.

After teaching English classes, I would walk the streets every day, trying to make a difference. Though my own resources were limited, people appreciated the fact that I was out there. I could not heal the sick, but I could pray for and comfort someone, and assure them of a better day. I did not have food for the hungry children each time, but I enjoyed singing songs with them and putting a smile on their faces. I discovered quickly that it was not what I had in terms of resources that made the difference. It was what I was able to give from my heart. They knew I cared about their concerns and issues. One day I met a father who had seven children and no job. I was not used to seeing a grown man beg for bread, or cry because he could not provide for his family. Neither was I prepared for the look on a mother's face when she knew her child was going to die from malaria, or the depressed young adults with college degrees who were cracking rocks for pennies a day because that was the only guaranteed income. Many felt better just knowing someone cared.

This is what happened to the woman with the hemorrhage, in Matthew 9:20-22. She knew what it was like to encounter Someone with purpose-guided compassion who truly cares. While everyone else distanced themselves and looked upon her as unclean, Jesus stood in her path because He cared about her condition. He saw pain and suffering every day, yet He did more than just heal. He provided spiritual, physical, and social freedom for those in circumstantial bondage. Just think what could happen in our world if everyone would add purpose-guided compassion to their personal "mission menu," and place themselves in the path to help someone in need.

God's got a plan, and your purpose-guided compassion is "IT" for someone.

Focus/Outcome: Everyone wants to see the end and know the results. One thing is for certain: God does not make mistakes. The scriptures say, "There is a way that seems right, but in the end is death." (Prov. 14:12) It is not pleasant to talk about devastating end results, but this is what God's plan can help you avoid. Some things in life you may not be able to control, but some things you can. What we plant now is what we will reap later.

Youth leaders spend many hours trying to help young people make right decisions, to guide them down the right path. Often the results are not so favorable. Some misjudge the outcome when ministering to someone with deep-rooted issues. We give up too soon because we forget that God is able to save anybody. Purpose-guided focus helps keep us anchored in God, knowing the outcome is always up to Him. We lead by faith, focusing on the eternal rather than the temporary. We walk by faith and not by sight.

I was invited to speak at a convention in Dallas, Texas, where I had ministered for 10 years. A young man who was a teenager when I left came up to say hello. He introduced his beautiful wife and baby. I told him I was proud of him, and how God had blessed in his life. He asked me if I was sincere in what I said. I assured him I was. Puzzled by his inquiry, I asked him later what he'd meant by that. He told me that he had been reluctant to approach me at first because I was aware of his teen issues, which were very critical. He feared that I thought worse of him. Stunned, I reassured him over and over that I never thought badly of him, that his present life was truly a blessing.

So many times we miss great opportunities because of distractions. Focus means just that: focus. If you dwell on the foolishness of how people feel about you, or who has not forgiven you, or what you have or don't have, you will definitely lose your focus. I am a firm believer that the present is always an opportunity, and I have a choice in what becomes of it. I can choose to stay focused on my goals and objectives in life; I can invest heavily in my next step towards increasing the significance of my influence.

I probably have a longer "To-Do List" than most people. It just keeps getting longer and longer! One might think that it is impossible to do all that's on it, but that's not my concern. You see, not only is it a long list, but I have it well organized, with timelines for each item. I also frequently check off tasks that have been completed. This gives me a sense of accomplishment and also allows me to grade my focus. I can truly say that I enjoy my "To-Do List." This is why I choose not to allow anything to distract me from what God has asked me to do. Set your eyes on the goal and run like mad towards it--not away from it. The only things you should run away from are the distractions: the unwelcome phone call that tries to drag you back into the past, the friends who don't share your values and vision, the relationship that is not good for you. All these only serve to compromise your focus. They have nothing to do with increasing the significance of your influence or strengthening you in God's plan for your life now. Purpose-guided focus means staying committed to the plan that God has for you.

God's Got a Plan and YoU're It!!!

Increasing the significance of your influence NOW

Chapter Three

My PRAYER:

Dear God,

I claim Your promise to purposefully guide me with directions, knowledge and understanding. I want to be purpose-guided in my intentions and efforts, my compassion and focus NOW. Please give me the guidance I need to know your will.

My PLAN:

From this day forward I will…

1.

2.

3.

4.

5.

6.

7.

Signature____

Date________________________

CHAPTER 4
PREPARE YOURSELF FOR THE PLAN

lay aside every weight...

Accomplishing anything good for God requires serious preparation. I have always been encouraged by the counsel in Hebrews 12:1: "Therefore we also, since we are surrounded by so great a cloud of witnesses, let us lay aside every weight, and the sin which so easily ensnares us, and let us run with endurance the race that is set before us." (KJV) God has a plan and you're "IT," so don't expect God to use you while you are half-stepping with unnecessary baggage.

I have always said that the quality of your **preparation** will determine the quality of your **performance.** Throughout history, God has always prepared His people, even when they did not know the plan. He knows where everything is headed. Everyone will be convinced one day that truly He is God. This is why it is so important to cooperate with His plan. We'll discuss some key areas to prepare:

a. Spiritually
b. Intellectually
c. Personal Growth
d. Socially
e. Physically

Prepare – Spiritually

There is a spiritual battle between good and evil over every soul. We have an enemy who works against God, and everything in the name of God. Jesus told Peter, "Simon, Simon! Indeed, Satan has asked for you, that he may sift you as wheat. But I have prayed for you, that your faith should not fail." (Luke 22: 31-32) Jesus was well aware of the spiritual battle, and called Peter's name twice (very uncharacteristically) to warn him. Preparing spiritually means connecting and staying tuned in to a personal relationship with God.

Daily personal devotion is a must for staying connected with God. We can talk about it all we want, but unless we actually make it a habit, we can lose touch with God in the plan. When something goes wrong in my life, I examine the consistency of my devotional life. Have I become so busy that I don't have time to spend with my Lord? I have discovered that there are 4 key components to my spiritual preparation and devotion to God:

1. A Consistent Prayer Life
2. Bible Study for Growth
3. Sharing my faith with others
4. Practicing what I believe

Prayer: I am convinced that prayer is the greatest preparation tool. There is something special about talking to Jesus. Talking to Him should be like talking to your best friend. Your best friend already knows everything about you anyway, so there is little you can hide. Talk to Jesus all the time. Tell Him everything. Include Him in everything. Even when doubts come, trust Him. My family once went through a trial so tremendous that I could not pray because I was so overwhelmed. I am not embarrassed to say this; it happens, whether we want to admit it or not. My faith was so weak at that time that I truly had to depend on the prayers of others. Then slowly but surely, I saw God begin the process of lifting the burden and working things out. That experience of depending on others' prayers taught me a valuable lesson: don't tell someone you are going to pray for them if you are not going to. They are depending on that prayer! Pray, then trust God to keep both you and the person you are praying for in perfect peace.

Jesus knew the importance of prayer when He led His disciples to the Garden of Gethsemane just before His trial and crucifixion. Several times He asked them to pray with Him, but sleep overcame them. Jesus begged and pleaded with His father for strength to bear the sacrifice for our sins. The end of the story confirms that prayer made a difference; Jesus is our Savior today!

Pray believing that God hears, and will answer your prayers according to His will. He is not going to allow you to be "IT" in His plan and not come through for you. After all, the plan belongs to Him anyway.

Bible Study: The second component in spiritual preparation is Bible study. Reading the Bible refreshes and elevates the soul. Reading about creation, the plan of salvation, God's precious promises, the life and teachings of Jesus--all are inspiring and deepen our faith in Him. The Psalmist declares in Psalm 119:105, "Your word is a lamp to my feet and a light to my path." I see the Word of God as my road map to an eternal destination. Sin hides the path so we cannot see it through the natural eye. As the Apostle says, "Spiritual things are spiritually discerned." (1 Cor. 2:14)

The thing I like best about reading the Word of God is that it's like watching a cliff-hanger movie. It appears as if God's people are losing, but then God says, "Watch this!" He allows them to be backed against a wall, trapped on all sides, like when Moses led the children of Israel out of Egypt. As they were being chased by Pharaoh and the Egyptian army, Israel had no place to run but forward by faith. The sea was before them and they could not turn back. The situation seemed impossible, but then God said, "Watch this!"

Moses declared, "Stand still and see the salvation of the Lord." (Ex. 14:13) Notice the command to "stand still." Sometimes God doesn't need you to do anything but stand still and see Him at work. Because of their obedience to the command, they crossed over on dry land. When I read this stuff in the Bible, it gives me the chills because of the awesomeness of God!

Take a front row seat and refresh yourself in the Word of God today. It's part of His plan for your life.

Sharing Your Faith: It's hard to keep a good thing to yourself. Get used to telling someone about the goodness of God. For me, sharing my faith is telling someone where I found the treasure chest of hope--there's so much there that anyone can get some. It's in my heart to see people experience the joy and happiness that I have found in Jesus. Perhaps nothing will increase the significance of your influence more than to look out for the best interest of another person.

Occasionally when I'm flying, I get into a conversation with a fellow passenger and they want to know what I do for a living. Eventually I start talking about my journey--how I am connected to God's plan, and all the awesome things He has done in my life. Also, I can share what I have seen God do in the lives of thousands of young people through the years. But most importantly, I share what God means to me. We can read, teach, sing, and talk about faith. "But what has He done for you?" That is the real question. Even if you don't feel you have a serious "come-to-Jesus" testimony, just tell what you know. Sometimes it's the simple things God has done in your life that will encourage people the most. When I give my testimony, people often want to exchange contact information so we can continue the dialogue. It's not so much that the influence of my testimony is that great. Rather, people are usually looking for something better than what they are currently experiencing. What's in it for me? The blessing goes both ways--to the giver and the receiver.

Practice what you believe: Perhaps you have heard it said that people would rather see a sermon than hear one any day. (Actually, I prefer both!) Nothing will kill your influence faster than being a hypocrite. A hypocrite is one who professes one thing but does another. Jesus says, "Therefore by their fruits you will know them." (Matt. 7:20) This was a serious problem in His day, and likewise today.

Through the years I have surveyed thousands of youth. The number one issue they have with Christians and the church is hypocrisy. These young people have lived long enough to have some idea of what it means to be faithful in Jesus. Of course many adults make the big mistake of assuming that kids don't know anything. But they know that the pastor and lead deacon are sleeping with the same person. They know that the choir director is a homosexual. They know that the head usher frequents a certain club every night, and the list goes on and on. Often the individuals in question are their parents.

Kids are wise enough to know the difference between perfection and living just as faithfully as you can. So I challenge you, young man and young lady: practice what you believe. Just because some do not care where they fit into God's plan does mean you should follow those poor examples. Never take for granted the spiritual preparation needed to be "IT" in God's plan. Always remember what Paul told Timothy, his young mentee: "Do not let anyone treat you as if you are unimportant because you are young. Instead, be an example to the believers with your words, your actions, your love, your faith, and your pure life." (1 Tim. 4:12, NCV)

Prepare – Intellectually

Preparing yourself in the plan requires intellectual preparation. Earlier I mentioned building up your personal library. The *United Negro College Fund* has a television commercial that says, "A mind is a terrible thing to waste." And I agree. The Bible says in Proverbs 1:5, "A wise man will hear and increase learning, and a man of understanding will attain wise counsel." The world is full of intelligent people, but sometimes they don't act like it. I read a quote once that said:

> "Whatever you hold in your mind will tend to occur in your life. If you continue to believe as you have always believed, you will continue to act as you have always acted. If you continue to act as you have always acted, you will continue to get what you have always gotten. If you want different results in your life or your work, all you have to do is change your mind." *(source unknown)*

So, how do we change our minds? "Let this mind be in you that was also in Christ…" (Phil. 2:5) Pray for the intelligence, mindset, and humility of Jesus.

I think of the decision Solomon faced as two mothers battled over the ownership of a child. I think of the difficult questions the Pharisees asked Jesus, and how He responded, both as a child and as an adult. Christ was intellectually prepared at all times. I think of the theological and social battles in the early church; the apostle Paul had to carefully navigate the issues in order for Jewish Christians and new believers to coexist in worship. Each of these examples shows the need for being intellectually prepared to handle the business of the day.

As a child, I remember the labels very well. There were the "smart" kids--and then the rest of us. I used to admire the "smart" kids; I even maintain relationships with many of them to this day. However, I am not as impressed by their "smarts" as I was when we were children. (No disrespect intended.) The fact is that intelligence is not about brains, it's about discipline. Do you have the discipline to learn, read, write, study, research, invest in resources, or set academic goals and reach them?
It was not until my second or third year in college that I realized that anyone can do those things if they apply themselves. The Bible says,

"Be diligent to present yourself approved to God, a worker who does not need to be ashamed, rightly dividing the word of truth." (2 Tim. 2:15) Faithful diligence will prepare you intellectually to be far beyond ordinary. God expects no less.

Each generation seems to get smarter and wiser, but not necessarily in spiritual things. The mind is like a sponge. It absorbs whatever you submerse it in. If you apply yourself, you can become an intelligent, useful agent for God in His plan.

Reading: It bothers me when someone says they hate to read. You don't have to like it, you just need to understand the importance of doing it. I encourage people to read as much as they can. Reading is a great habit to form. Books (all forms), magazines, articles, newspapers, etc. are excellent for building vocabulary and intellect. Readers don't have to take someone else's word for anything; they can read it for themselves. It always fascinates me to observe people in the audience when I'm preaching. When I mention a scripture, some will turn to it immediately, while others don't even have their Bibles open. They are content with taking my word for it. Maybe I should feel flattered, but I don't.

As a creative way of getting young people involved in reading the Bible, I often have a Bible-reading marathon activity during my conventions and retreats. The young people really enjoy this, and it gives a fresh perspective on the Word of God.

Reading may be difficult for you or someone you know. But getting help in this area may be the best thing you ever did. It can give you the tools to take control of your own life. Reading researchers have found that. . .

- Students may need to encounter an unfamiliar word six times in context before they have enough experience to understand and recall its meaning. (Jenkins, Stein, & Wysocki, 1984)

- Three potential stumbling blocks can throw children off course on the journey to skilled reading:

    1. Difficulty understanding and using the alphabetic principle (the idea that written spellings systematically represent spoken words)

    2. Failure to transfer the comprehension skills of spoken language to reading and to acquire new strategies that may be specifically needed for reading

    3. Absence of motivation to read or failure to develop a mature appreciation of the rewards of reading (Snow, Burns, & Griffin, 1998)

It is unfortunate (but not surprising) that many children and adults read at an alarmingly low rate. How will they discover new things if they can't read? Many have learned how to fake it and get by. This is a very sensitive area for me, because my siblings and I taught our father how to read, speaking aloud the words he could not pronounce. He grew up in a time when all family members had to work the fields just to eat, and completing the third grade was considered a decent level of education. We were inspired that he spent so much time in books and magazines, despite not knowing all the words. Every time we went into a store, Daddy would go directly to the book/magazine section and read the entire time Mother was shopping. Later, my siblings and I started to do the same thing. Instead of running around the store like other little kids, we were reading magazines--or at least looking at the pictures.

Another reason the reading issue is close to my heart is because of my experience in Haiti. As a student missionary, I witnessed the discipline of poverty-stricken individuals who were eager to learn. Learning to read was part of their plan for getting out of poverty. The books were often old with torn pages, but the students valued every word.

You are in God's plan, so set a goal that you will read a book a week, or a book a month, or every two months. Just read!

Listening: This skill is also valuable in preparing intellectually. Listening is not the same as hearing. Hearing is one of our five senses, listening is a skill. Someone who is hearing-impaired can be a great listener if they pay attention to the information someone conveys to them, regardless of how it is being communicated. Likewise, someone with very sharp hearing can be a poor listener if they do not attend to what is being communicated. Listening involves more than just hearing the words that are directed towards us. It is how we make sense of, assess, and respond to what we hear. This skill is important in all our relationships because when we listen to each other, we show that we care. Mastering the art of listening is truly vital.

If you will observe, you will discover that many people of influence listen well. Listening was part of the plan that got them where they are now. Often we miss much because we are not listening to people. We hear them, but we are not listening. God wants you to have empathy: to hear the cry of those who are discouraged, to hear the baby crying to be picked up, to hear the teenager trying to tell you something, to hear the desperate just trying to survive, to hear the voice of God saying "this is the right path, so take it." (Is. 30:21)

"Listen to advice and accept correction, and in the end you will be wise." (Prov. 19:20, NCV) Just think--you can build your intellect and your influence in God's plan by simply listening.

As a counselor, many times I am not sure how to respond to people's problems, but listening provides some of the tools I need to help them work out their situation. Often I review with them what I heard them say until we discover the right solution together. I remember a time when I needed help from a counselor, but did not get the same benefit.

I knew she was not giving me her undivided attention, although she was looking right at me. When she offered a plan for me to consider, it was totally off base. I concluded that she had heard what she wanted to, not what I was saying.

Nature provides an excellent opportunity for sharpening your listening skills. Just sit still wherever you are; listen and describe what you hear. You may hear birds singing, a gurgling creek, wind in the trees, or maybe God speaking silently.

Seek counsel: No one knows it all, but some of us think we do. God's plan is huge and there is so much He wants to do through you. Seeking counsel of those who have more experience and are better qualified is a great practice. This does not suggest that you lack a mind of your own, but rather indicates that you value the wisdom of others. "Listen to counsel and receive instruction, that you may be wise in your latter days." (Prov. 19:20)

I have to admit that over the years I have received some bad counsel; I have also (unintentionally) given some bad counsel. It is important to ask God to guide you to the right people for counsel or advice. Avoid those who feel their counsel is the gospel. I usually get counsel from someone I trust and admire, or who has a pretty good track record for success. As a young person, your parents--if they are stable--should ideally be your first counselors. They know you best and will not guide you wrong, because they want most of all to see you succeed and become a person of significant influence for God. For others it may be a family member, a trusted friend or co-worker. Just make certain you process any counsel you receive to determine whether it is actually best for you. Most importantly, try to seek counsel from those who are guided by God.

There is a myth that seeking counsel is a sign of weakness. Nothing could be further from the truth! When someone's life is dependent upon your actions, you want to make certain you are heading in the right direction. As a writer, I generally share a book manuscript with about a dozen persons of various backgrounds, just to get their thoughts before I make anything public. Getting counsel provides a safeguard against prejudice and narrow-mindedness.

What is the best counsel you've ever received? I know what mine was. It came from my father years ago. Because I spent most of my growing-up years as the only boy in the family (I lost my brother at age 17), Dad made certain that I was prepared for life. He told me that I should not only prepare myself mentally for life's challenges, but also that I should learn a trade that could always bring me an income. In other words, use both my head and my hands. He said if I did that, I would never go hungry. Daddy had been hungry a few times in his life, but learning to work hard and developing skills in various areas took care of that problem.

Because of his counsel, I spent three years in high school learning the masonry trade. I learned the industrial art of brick laying very well; I could lay more brick and block per hour than anyone else in the class. I would create various designs and find shortcuts to save money in building them. Having a trade gave me an added sense of confidence. Interestingly, I have never made a living laying bricks, but I am able to use that skill in various volunteer projects, and train others to do the same. Remember, even if your career takes a different path than the trade you learned, you can still use those skills to help yourself and others. Just imagine the influence you could have if you opened a business, hired your own crew, and were able to help those less fortunate than yourself!

The purpose of counsel is to help you make the right decision. Counsel is not the decision. Only you can make those life decisions. Again, as I said before, process everything carefully, then give it to God and He will guide you as He builds your intellect in the plan. Seeking good counsel in God's plan will increase the significance of your influence NOW.

Expand Mental Territory: Don't be afraid to expand your mental territory. Certainly you want to protect your mind from things that may be harmful, but don't be afraid to broaden your capacity for learning. Sudoku, Bible bowls, trivia games, crossword puzzles, brain teasers, etc.--such exercises can help you think more sharply, recall information faster when you need it, and keep your mind active.

One of my favorite mental exercises is observing people. It's interesting to watch them. As part of a project, I once spent two days just watching people in the parks and subways of Midtown Manhattan. Of course I had to be discreet, but I left with a wealth of information. In just a few hours I was able to recognize people who were happy, angry, mad, confused, psychotic, focused, determined, criminal, curious, lost, excited, overwhelmed, worried or hopeless. There is so much to learn by just observing.

Travel is another means of expanding mental alertness. See the world if you can. People who have not had the opportunity to travel are often limited in their scope of thinking. Several years ago, I was assigned my first leadership role in my church organization. This immediately opened up a variety of traveling opportunities. I was living in Texas at the time, and had to attend a meeting in Alberta, Canada. While there, I went with friends to visit Banff National Park--a camper's dream. There the glacier touches the beautiful, turquoise, tranquil Lake Louise. Nestled between mountains and surrounded by Canadian pines, my first impression was of breath-taking beauty. It is an unbelievable sight. That trip made an indelible impression on me; I realized immediately that I had to see more of the world, and that I would use my influence to help others do so as well.

As a youth ministries director, I determined to challenge the youth to go outside of their comfort zones. I organized several large trips that changed the lives of many and taught them about taking responsibility. The first one involved taking 500 young people on a 7,000-mile journey from the Southwest region of the United States to Canada. Of course, our first stop was Lake Louise in Banff National Park. That trip also included Glacier National Park, Salt Lake City, the Grand Canyon and the Petrified Forest. We made history, because up to that point we were the largest single group to ever hike all those areas!

Just imagine what the trip did for those young people. Certainly there was an assignment at each location along the way. This stretched their brains like nothing else. Everyone's journal was full of "WOW factors" that made a lasting impression on them. When I travel throughout North America and different parts of the world, I see some of those youth--now adults--and many of them still talk about that trip.

So as you prepare for God's plan, get out see the world--or at least the nearest state park. Go to a museum, or an aquarium with various species of creatures from around the world. Personally, I feel tremendously blessed, honored and humbled to have traveled so much of the world sharing the good news of my Lord and Savior, Jesus Christ. We have much to gain from experiencing other people and their cultures. Learning something in each place that you visit positions you to become an extraordinary influence for those in need. Having "been there and done that" helps make you the "IT" in God's plan.

Prepare – Personal Growth

Grow every area of your life: God said to Adam and Eve, "be fruitful and multiply." (Gen. 1:28) Although He was referring to procreation, He also wants us to "be fruitful and multiply" in the area of personal growth. You are a beautiful creation in His plan. You were born to blossom. Your life is like a freshly-planted garden. You must take care of it. You will need nurturing, cultivating, water, sunshine and occasional weeding in order to become the fully-grown person He plans to use to bless yourself and others.

My grandparents had a large farm with lots of areas under cultivation. Something was always growing. I never saw them plant the seeds, but we were always there for the harvest. I remember picking watermelons, soy beans, corn, cotton, peanuts, and potatoes. There was a spirit about harvest time that I will never forget. Though we were all sweating like crazy, everybody seemed happy. I learned later that this was because everyone was getting paid. This is how you should view your personal growth. If you plant seeds in your life now, you will reap a harvest later. Reaping means getting paid--but not always with money, although we want that too. Personal growth means getting paid spiritually, socially, emotionally, physically, academically, professionally, and financially.

To be influential in God's plan you must grow every area of your life. You are a work in progress. Like the harvest, it won't happen overnight, so be patient. Allow room for growth and give yourself time to be all you can be. Some of the greatest wonders of the world took decades to build. For instance, the Leaning Tower of Pisa took 120 years to build, and St. Peter's Basilica in Rome was under construction for 176 years. Don't settle for less than you are worth. Know that you are priceless, worth the wait.

Value every aspect of life: the good and the not-so-good. Continually evaluate your personal growth plan. Don't ever get to the point where you feel you are done. The journey God is planning for you is for the long term, so you have to pay attention to all the details as you develop various areas. Don't depend on anyone else to do this for you. You are responsible for yourself. Personal growth is just that, PERSONAL GROWTH. It's personal, so you have to do it yourself. No one but you can take responsibility for growing you. You have to take charge of what is best for you. There is only one of you, so by God's grace, invest in making the most of yourself. Doing this is not meant to be selfish; instead it is helping you be the best YOU in God's plan. Being the best you can will reward you with influence beyond your imagination, because those you serve may want to become like you. I am not sure about you, but if someone looks up to me, I want them to become what Christ has been to me. I trust my Christian growth more than my natural side. One thing I have learned through Christ: if you are valuable to yourself, you will be valuable to others. Jesus became the perfect sacrifice so I could live.

Balance: Balance is a major component in life's journey. I love watching a gymnast on the balance beam. They are never in a hurry; they take their time, and they are extremely focused. When I was a child we used to play on the see-saw. One person on each end of a board, trying to balance. We would go up and down, up and down. Occasionally, despite the weight discrepancies, we would succeed. Balance slows things down and makes you appreciate the journey. Some people take everything nonstop; these folks often achieve little because they lack balance, which leads to confusion in life. We've all heard the saying that too much of anything can be harmful. Find your balance.

Have you ever wondered why some business deals take place on the golf course, in restaurants, at resorts or someplace other than the business office? It's because tension can be a deal-breaker. Smart business people who build great relationships know when to have fun and when to be serious. They know that great relationships are multifaceted; they require adapting to each situation, and the people in it. This helps create balance among the parties, and may afford an opportunity to see the sensitivity or complexity of a deal through another set of eyes. The ability to create and maintain balance can increase your significance in God's plan.

Perhaps you got off to a great start in the balance department--then everything went wrong. Refocus and get back on the balance beam. Falling off does not mean you are disqualified. You don't even have to start over, you just continue. After all, life is not about perfect scores. It's about achieving structure and balance in your life. Have fun--stand back and look at the full picture of your daily life. Go ahead: take a break, take a vacation, enjoy some family time, and make some new friends. These suggestions can contribute to adequate balance in your personal growth and increase the significance of your influence in God's plan.

Challenge yourself: Be your own coach and push yourself to the limit. Remember, you are preparing in God's plan! I enjoy watching the reality show, *The Biggest Loser*. The thing I appreciate most about this show is its focus on helping people who have faced great obstacles in their lives, and in some cases, life-threatening health challenges. The trainers encourage, motivate, and push these individuals to the limit. However, there some things the trainers cannot do for the participants. They cannot lift weights for someone, run, breathe, or keep them from eating certain foods that are not good for the plan.

Each participant is taught how to take care of themselves by focusing on a goal and seeing it through. They have to push themselves to the limit. They cry, sweat, fall down, argue, and complain, but the routine remains the same. The trainers are focused on one thing: helping them lose the weight. Those who are most successful are those who realize right away that they have to do it for themselves. Once they are convinced of this, they work with unstoppable ambition to lose the weight. At the end of each week there is the weigh-in, the time of revelation. Contestants all wait anxiously, wondering how much weight they have lost. Sometimes the loss is significant; other times it may be minimal, none at all, or the occasional weight gain. God's plan is no different from *The Biggest Loser.* He stands right by our side, encouraging, motivating and pushing us to the limit with trials and tribulations, preparing us for the weigh-in.

Although I have never participated in a triathlon, I enjoy watching them. The discipline that is required for training seems awfully strenuous. At least that's what I thought until I talked to a friend of mine in

Fort Worth, Texas, who participated in one several years ago. He told me that the more he trained, the **easier** it got. The real pain begins when you advance from one level to the next.

Many people do not push themselves to the next level in life. Challenging yourself should become routine. Don't worry about the person next to you or the one ahead of you. Just clock your own time. Always aim to become better than your best. Setting realistic long- and short-term goals is a great beginning to realizing how far you can go. Set the standard high, then aim to break your own record. Just don't give up and do the best you can. Some of the best things in life require persistence and hard work. After you have pushed and challenged yourself to the limit, be sure to double check.

As you challenge yourself, avoid the "good enough" syndrome. Accept the fact that "good enough" will never be enough. Unless we challenge ourselves, we will never reach the optimum potential in God's plan and our influence will always be less than it could be.

God's got a plan and you're "IT"!

Finances: God's plan for your life is not complete without a thorough understanding of the world of personal finance. I have learned much about finance through years of trial and error, and I'm convinced that if you respect your budget, your budget will respect you. You should be able to articulate your personal philosophy about money, and how it can work for you. You must also have a biblical understanding of what God requires of you in His plan.

Make a financial plan. It begins with a JOB--a means of earning an honest income. **Then make a budget.** A good budget will help you reach your short- and long-term financial goals. List all the things that are necessary and important for managing your personal economy. Certainly God is number one, because without Him you have nothing.

Honor Him with your tithe, then give an offering. Years ago, my family and I started out with 10% tithe and 5% offering. As our financial security grew, we increased our offerings significantly. Some people do not give much to the church because they feel that all the church wants is your money. Well, I believe that I give to God through the church. Everyone, including those leaders who are responsible for managing what has been given to the church, is held accountable by God. I trust His promise that if I am faithful to God, He will be faithful to me. In Malachi 3:10, God says, "I am the Lord All-Powerful, and I challenge you to put me to the test. Bring the entire ten percent into the storehouse, so there will be food in my house. Then I will open the windows of heaven and flood you with blessing after blessing." (CEV). Now, that's a challenge I am willing to take. That's a plan!

As you build (or rebuild) your plan, here are some additional tips that I have found to be helpful in creating financial stability:

1. Live within your means. You may have heard this pithy saying: "If your outgo exceeds your income, then your upkeep will be your downfall!" (Bill Earle)

2. **Pay your obligations on time.**

3. Make certain you pay yourself and **save regularly.**

4. **Avoid the debt trap.** The best way to do this is to live within your means. Be content with what you have and don't be distracted by what others have.

5. Other than purchasing a home, learn to pay cash for what you need.

6. Only use credit when absolutely necessary.

7. Avoid carrying credit card balances--paying only the minimum due is a trap.

8. Have a spending plan--don't spend every day.

9. Avoid TV shopping programs (infomercials) and the internet-only sales that offer items you think you need.

God wants to use you to be a blessing to others, but debt and mismanagement can derail that plan. Financial freedom can help you help others.

This is a very sensitive area for my family and me, because we went through a period of time with our finances when I wondered where God was. Of course, He was right where He's always been. Instead of trying to find a way out of our situation, I was complaining about how we got into it. I realized then, and still believe today, that if there was a way in, there is also a way out. I am a firm believer that everyone should have an entrepreneurial spirit. Just like my trade in masonry, I can use what I have get where I want to go financially.

At the risk of being misunderstood, I offer this personal example. All my life I have loved animals; dogs are my favorite. I've had all kinds of dogs: stray dogs, no-name dogs, dogs who thought they were mine, but mostly German Shepherds--until now. In recent years, my family and partners have invested in breeding English Bulldogs, with the goal of using any profits to provide opportunities for parolees. It has been a serious challenge for us, while at the same time it's been a blessing for those who are seeking a second chance. We decided to raise high-quality purebred dogs. We have learned that when you have a proven product, you don't have to negotiate, and there will always be a waiting list. So unless your budget will permit you to spend $2,500-$3,500 per dog, don't bother contacting www.metropridebulldogs.com. We have volunteers and parolees that provide exceptional care for our brood. Some may think, wow--what a great opportunity! Don't be fooled; while it may eventually pay off, we have been picking up dog poop every day since 1987.

There is no doubt that people with money have significant influence. However, as you prepare for God's plan, try to avoid both the "greed mentality" and the "prosperity gospel." I know that some people will do anything to become rich. But you should know, there is a big difference between wealth and financial freedom. If God brings wealth your way, praise Him. If you have to lie, steal or cheat for the money, it is not from God. It will eventually destroy you, and everything around you. We've seen too many examples of how wealth destroyed talented lives. Think of Howard Hughes, Michael Jackson, Whitney Houston and many others who seemed to have had everything but happiness. The rich young ruler wanted to be in Jesus' plan, but he would not sell all that he had and give to the poor. In other words, he chose his financial wealth over God's plan of eternal riches for his life.

God has a plan for you, and it's not made of lottery tickets and scams. It may be computer repair on the side, landscaping in the evening, a small home bakery that targets specific clients. (I live in the DC area, and I like whole-wheat raisin bread. Hint, hint!) It may be face-painting for birthday parties or balloon art in the park, real estate or an internet business. Find out what works for you and use it to complement what you are already doing. Remember, there is a way in and there is a way out. It is hard to increase the significance of your influence when you are broke all the time.

Discipline and patience are key elements in managing your economy. You work hard for your money; why not manage it just as hard? God wants to use you in His plan to bless others. How much money can He trust you with?

God has a plan and you're "IT"!

Education: Thousands of people have used education as a ticket to discovering their calling in life. As a young African-American living in West Savannah, Georgia, I truly believe that I would not have the life I now live, if I hadn't left to go to college in 1976. Today my life is focused on serving people and being a mentor to many.

Education is not optional today. We are all students in the school of life. No matter your age, you are never too young to pursue higher goals, and you are never too old to go back to school in preparation for God's plan. It is true that not everyone who finishes high school and college gets the job they had in mind, but the chances are always better with a higher education. Educating yourself may also mean attending professional workshops and taking online courses. Dozens of free seminars are available every day, for the purpose of introducing people to cutting-edge technology, or new industries, products and services. Just take advantage of every opportunity you can.

Several years ago, my wife Maxine and a friend went to Columbia, South Carolina for grant writing training. At the end of this 5-day course, participants received certification. For years now, Maxine has written successful grants for small organizations and brought countless blessings to their communities.

Maybe you already have this part figured out, and you have all the education you need. If this is the case, then inspire someone else. You may not be able to pay someone's full tuition, but write one of those "I-am-thinking-of-you" checks today, and send it to someone you know in college.

Apply yourself: If you are a student (or planning to go back to school), apply yourself in the classroom like you're on a mission for God. He is preparing you for greatness, so you have to know what you are talking about. Sit at the front of the class; always have a study plan; practice taking good, organized notes; know what the teacher is expecting; ask questions if you don't understand. Make up your own test before an exam, and don't wait until the last minute to start studying. I discovered something that worked for me in graduate school; I wish I had learned it in undergrad. When I took ownership of the material--acted like I was teaching it myself--I was able to master it, because it became mine. On several occasions, my instructors complimented me for adding subject material that they had not presented. Because of my own research, the additions were accurate.

Personal growth in education means it's never over. There's always another level, and you get there one class at a time. In God's plan you can be an advocate for education.

Attitude: We've all met them, the customer service representatives with nasty attitudes. They don't greet you, they don't ask if you've found everything you need. They don't make eye contact; they chew gum while helping you, and on top of all that, they have the audacity to answer their cell phone while they're supposed to be assisting you! Their entire persona says "I don't want to be here. You're just an annoyance to me."

Your attitude is more than altitude and latitude. It's the introduction to who you are. A person with a negative attitude does not attract many friends. Negativity tends to breed negativity.

You want to grow the right attitude. A positive attitude will always yield something good, because positivity breeds positivity. Take time to evaluate your attitude, and how it will be perceived. My late father, John Black, and my mother, Claretha, always had positive attitudes. Dad rarely complained about anything and had lots of friends. He and my mother were always invited to social occasions. People loved to see them coming. Although my mother is alone today--John Black died in 2005 at age 83--her attitude is still positive. She always has something good to say.

Another aspect of attitude is the contrast between **response** and **reaction.** How you respond to the simplest things demonstrates your attitude. Some people react with an overdose of emotions, while others respond by thinking things through and coming up with a plan. Recently, a friend tried to contact me, and said he needed to talk. I thought it was in reference to a ministry product he was representing. He kept calling, and I kept avoiding his calls. Because I could not honestly give him my support, I did not want to hurt his feelings. He even came to a conference where I was speaking. I barely had time for him, yet he insisted, "I need to talk to you ASAP."

The following week, I was sitting in my office when my administrative assistant said that Marcus was calling. She asked if I wanted to take the call. I decided to get it over with, so I grudgingly picked up the phone. When I answered, Marcus was so grateful. We had a few minutes of small talk, then he shared his reason for wanting to talk to me. When he finished, we both were in tears--he because he was hurting badly, I because I'd ignored his pain for about four months. Due to my attitude, I'd almost missed a moment in God's plan to use my influence to bring healing to a friend who needed me. I felt stupid for weeks, and asked God and my friend to forgive me for neglecting my duty. The wrong attitude can rob us of many opportunities to increase the significance of our influence in God's plan.

Personal growth is not complete without a positive, healthy attitude. God's plan is for you to encourage and cheer others with a great attitude.

Don't accept partial growth: Some may think that none of this applies to them. But God wants you to be complete in His plan. I have never liked the word "partial." To me, it's a scary word. If my life were to depend on someone who only finished partial training, I'd say, "Please do not touch me! I will pray and ask God to find a ram in the bushes to help me!"

Consider these examples of jobs only partially completed: the surgeon who neglects to stitch up his patient; the plumber who shows up, but fails to stop the leak; an electrician who forgets to turn the power off (or back on!); a teacher who doesn't show up for class; a cook who has no knives, or the pilot who fails to let down the landing gear on YOUR flight!

Nature blossoms every year. It doesn't quit after a successful springtime. When you think you have achieved, grow some more--you are going to be awesome if you follow the plan. Nothing half-baked is ready to be served. Continuous and complete personal growth is the goal. Set a standard for achievement and measure yourself by it. Go all the way; half the distance won't do. God needs full-grown individuals with influence to carry out His plan, and you are one of them.

Prepare – Socially

When I was in elementary school, my report card had a category for "citizenship" listed on it. I was confused about it until my teacher explained that it meant how we get along with others. Most times I had a failing grade. I tried to do better, but Calvin Brown kept messing with me and I had to defend myself! I should have passed, though. That could have been an easy grade.

What's your grade in citizenship? This is not about immigration status, but about how well you get along with others. Do people like being around you? How well do you serve others? What is your personal weather forecast? Is it cold, warm, cloudy, sunshiny, rainy, foggy? Are the winds calm, pleasant, or thunderous? It does not take much to grow into a good citizen. You only need to be mindful of others around you. Treat them as you want to be treated.

My wife Maxine is able to do something that I admire. You know how cold society can be sometimes--people pass right by you and don't speak. This often happens in church on a weekly basis. You might be dying on the street, and no one would dial 9-1-1. A person might be attacked in broad daylight, but no one calls the police.

Well, my wife speaks to everyone, but what she does on an elevator beats me. People generally don't speak to strangers in a public elevator. But Maxine will see a dozen people in a packed elevator, and speak to each one like she sees them every day. And if they don't respond the first time, she will speak louder to make certain everyone heard. I must confess, I cannot do that and I'm often embarrassed when she does it. I have shared my concerns about this with her several times, but obviously I have no significant influence with her on this matter!

In places that we visit regularly, some of those people will see her and wave; they may even walk over to say hello, and talk briefly. That might be the extent of the interaction, and that's okay. But for those few moments, Maxine transcends the stranger/stranger relationship and brightens someone's day. Great citizenship means treating every relationship, no matter how minor and fleeting, as if it has value—after all, in God's sight it does.

Society needs more people to practice good citizenship. If you present yourself with excellent citizenship skills, you might get that unexpected recommendation or promotion. You might be surprised by that award next month. People generally like seeing in others what they don't see in themselves. Good citizenship is one of the best ways to increase the significance of your influence in God's plan NOW.

Diversity: Personal growth in the area of diversity is something many people don't want to talk about. How do you see the world? Is there enough for everyone, or do you cater to your own kind? The world is more beautiful when you treat everyone equally well, regardless of gender, race, ethnicity, religion, class, preferences, differences, etc. Sometimes people think that accepting diversity means we all have to agree. Nothing is further from the truth. Understanding diversity and being part of a diverse community means that God is preparing me for the next level.

Jesus chose a diverse group of disciples. Although he did not have a woman on his team (that we know about), Jesus treated women with respect and made it clear He had no problem dealing with them. The woman who was hemorrhaging for 12 years, the Samaritan woman at the well, Mary Magdalene, and even the importunate Canaanite mother--these illustrate how Jesus embraced diversity. He separated Himself from no one. Sometimes this means going against the grain.

One way to test your influence is to see if your friends know where you stand on the issues. Is it ok for them to make crude jokes about the other sex around you? Are racial cracks a part of men's night out? If you are a Christian, do you have Muslim friends? Where do you stand on the issue of women in ministry? Are your children allowed to play with the neighbors? Who do you hang out with? Does everyone at your parties look alike?

It is easy to say that diversity is part of our wardrobe, but do we wear it well when it's needed? The best form of diversity is that which is practiced, not talked about. I am the first African-American to hold the position of national youth ministries director for my church. Because I serve more than 6,000 churches in the United States, Canada and Bermuda, I was once asked if I had experienced any prejudice during my 11-year journey. I was able to answer truthfully that I had not. Besides, if there is any, I don't have time for it! My goal is to draw people to a saving knowledge of Jesus Christ. All I know is that any given weekend, I may see hundreds of kids at the altar, weeping in surrender to Christ.

That's what matters. My point here is that even if diversity is foreign to some of the people around me, it does not have to affect the significance of my influence in God's plan.

Go ahead, champion--the world can't wait to meet you! Anyone who desires to grow with God will cherish the importance of personal growth in the area of diversity. It's needed in God's plan.

Build Relationships: One who builds relationships will never be alone. God does not call you to work in a vacuum. You must build relationships in order to be prepared socially. Cultivating a wide variety of relationships is like having acres of building supplies. As you build, you can reach out and find what you need to get the job done. Just choose one of those relationships you established last year. People want to help you make a difference when you honor your relationships.

Look around you; what don't you have? There was a time in my ministry when I did not have many non-Christian friends or acquaintances. It seemed like everyone I knew well was in Christian circles. During my time as a pastor in Amarillo, Texas, I met a gentleman who worked out at the gym when I did. One day in the course of conversation, I asked him about his faith. He said he was not much of a believer. So I asked him what he thought about Christians. His response stuns me to this day. He said he did not think very highly of Christians, because we seem to be stuck on ourselves. That opinion had to have come from something in his experience. I told him that I was sorry for the image, and hoped one day it could change. I invited him to our church, where the members showered him with love and affection.

Recently my wife and I returned to Amarillo for a mortgage-burning celebration. Guess who met us at the door: my friend Greg, from the gym! I had no idea he had been back to the church after I moved away from Amarillo. We talked as if I'd never left, although he left out some of what used to happen on the basketball court!

Building relationships will extend your influence far beyond your expectations. Each relationship you establish multiplies your usefulness in God's plan.

Prepare – Physically

How long do you want to be the "IT" in God's plan? How many years do you want to be around for your family? I want to be available to God for the long term. In order to do that, I must establish good health habits.

Diet/Nutrition: I used to love potato chips. An old television commercial bragged, "No one can eat just one." Don't try that if you are really hungry, because it's hard to resist those delicious salty morsels. The truth, is potato chips are junk food. And junk food will produce junk health. We are what we eat; most people eat just about everything. According to the *American Journal of Clinical Nutrition*, more than one third of American adults--more than 72 million people--and 16% of children in the United States are obese. The 2011 *Nurses' Health Study* published in the *New England Journal of Medicine* listed foods that contribute the most to weight gain: French fries, potato chips, sugar-sweetened drinks, red meats and processed meats, sweets and desserts, refined grains, fried foods, 100% fruit juice, and butter. A 2011 study conducted by the Centers for Disease Control and Prevention found that the average male consumes 175 calories a day from drinks containing added sugar (like soda). The average female consumes 94 calories from these drinks, and about half of the population drinks a sugar-sweetened beverage on any given day.

The Bible says that our bodies are the temple of the Holy Spirit. We must treat our bodies like the dwelling of God. We would not fill God's church with junk and trash; neither should we place just anything in our bodies. Many of today's health issues are the result of poor investment in health.

Educate yourself in healthy eating and good lifestyle choices. Eat balanced meals daily and eat in moderation. Nuts, grains, vegetables, fruits, and legumes--this was the original diet that allowed man to live for hundreds of years after Creation. A good multi-vitamin helps, but can't replace a healthy diet.

Annual Doctor/Dentist Visits: Don't wait until you are sick to go to the doctor. Get regular checkups. Many people are more concerned about their car maintenance than their health. A dental visit makes some folks nervous, but having no teeth makes me extremely nervous!

Exercise: In my humble opinion, the best exercise is the one we enjoy the most. Do something; your body is worth it! I would love to be a long distance runner, but a daily walk of several miles or a bicycle ride is sufficient for me. Stretching is beneficial as well. Make exercise part of your daily life.

Water: Water is life; drink 6-8 glasses a day. Someone told me that they don't drink much water because it makes them go to the restroom too often. Well, that's the whole idea! Flushing purifies. How often do you flush? The body builds up many types of toxins, and water is a natural cleanser. There is no substitute for pure water--the best medicine for the human body.

Fresh Air: I appreciate fresh air much more after spending a week in Mumbai, India. The pollution was so bad there that by the end of the day, I experienced a deep burning sensation in my chest. I could barely breathe. Days later, we went out to Pune to visit Spicer College. Pune is located in the countryside with plenty of fresh air. Amazingly, my breathing improved immediately. Practice deep breathing exercises daily in fresh air for a clear mind in God's plan.

Nature: It's a great place to be! Find some quiet time with God in nature. Have you ever noticed how children's behavior changes when they're outside? It's as if the outdoors was made just for them. The freedom to play and discover is energizing. When I need perspective, I usually reflect on some of the most beautiful scenes I've encountered around the world: the Grand Canyon, Glacier National Park, Banff National Park, Hawaii Coast, Serengeti National Park, the countryside of Thailand, Taiwan, Australia and New Zealand. Find your special place in nature and listen to God as He shares His plan for your life.

God's Got a Plan and YoU're It!!!

Increasing the significance of your influence NOW

Chapter Four

My PRAYER:

Dear God,

I want to prepare myself spiritually, intellectually, and with personal growth. What is Your significant plan for my life NOW? Please give me the guidance I need to know Your will.

My PLAN:

From this day forward I will…

1.

2.

3.

4.

5.

6.

7.

Signature____

Date________________________

CHAPTER 5

POSITION YOURSELF FOR THE PLAN

there is a lad

Perhaps you have read the story found in Matthew 14:15-21, about Jesus preaching to a multitude of people just before the Passover. Thousands had gathered to hear Him; after many hours, Jesus knew the people were hungry and needed to eat. He told His disciples to feed the crowd--but as they pointed out, that would require an awful a lot of money. One of them found a boy who had a sack lunch: five barley loaves and two small fish. You might think like the disciples did--they asked, "What are these among so many?" In essence, how could this little bit of food possibly feed all these people? Obviously, Jesus was not positioning for the "how" but the "NOW."

That little boy had been precisely placed in God's plan. He was in the right spot at the right time. I am impressed that he worked his way close to Jesus, not even knowing God was going to use him in the plan. The fact that he was the only one with a lunch says something about his thinking. Since it was just before the Passover feast, the day would be long and there were crowds of people. I am certain the lines were slow at the marketplace. He had to be visible in order for the disciple to know he had a lunch. When people are hungry, they may not see you, but they will see your food. Lastly, the boy was willing to share his lunch: if needed, I'm here!

Again, it was not about how much, but about what God can do with whatever we have, once we willingly position ourselves in His plan. The obvious miracle is that over 20,000 people enjoyed an all-you-can-eat buffet. But for me, the greater miracle is that 12 baskets of leftovers showed up out of nowhere. After everyone had eaten, it was apparent that one little boy's unselfish generosity, coupled with the blessings of the Master, positioned him as "IT" in God's plan. Do you think there was an increase in the significance of his influence? Absolutely!

Position Your Availability: Every day is an interview for a POSITION in God's plan. Currently, thousands of people are jobless because of the recent recession in the United States. Finding a job can be a daunting experience even when you are qualified. And there may be only one position open, with 5,000 applicants. Nevertheless, you don't know whether you can get the job unless you apply for it. You just might be the one in 5,000.

If you get hired, the first thing your employer wants to know is, when you can start? If you're like me when I first got hired at the Piggly Wiggly store in Garden City, Georgia, your responses might go something like this:

When can you start? I can start NOW!

What shifts can you work? Any of them.

Are you willing to work overtime? Yes.

Can you…? Yes, yes, YES!

A friend of mine got the job he always wanted--then called in sick several times during the first couple of weeks. Management called him in to remind him that the first 90 days were a probationary period. He got well in record time.

Positioning your availability is critical to increasing your influence. This means no one has to go looking for you--you're right there. Years ago my parents advised my siblings and me to keep emergency change in our pockets, in case we had to use a pay phone to call for help. Nowadays, you can hardly find a pay phone. Cell phones have changed the way business is done. E-mail is passé; texting and FaceTime are the modes of the day. However, few things will damage your position more than giving someone your cell number--and never answering your phone when they call.

I have to admit, this drives me nuts. You are walking around with the phone; everyone knows you have the phone on you, but you never seem to answer it or listen to your messages. That means you also don't return calls. This sends a clear message to your contacts that you are not available. Certainly there are times when you really SHOULD turn off your phone. But never picking up a call tells people that you cannot be counted upon for doing business.

I try to respond to people in a timely manner, and I value having a reputation for following through. I enjoy hearing people say that I am easy to reach. I choose to position my availability carefully, because the next call could be another opportunity in God's plan for me.

God wants to impact someone's life using you as His instrument. Start positioning your availability now.

Position Your Integrity: Our gifts, talents, and skills may vary, but our integrity should be constant. As you prepare to be "IT" in God's plan, you must understand that integrity is a requirement, not an option. If we simply took our cues from the news, we might think that it's ok to be dishonest in order to achieve instant gratification. After all, it seems that the people who cut corners and deceive others are getting ahead. If there is one value to live by, this is it: integrity is forever. It means doing the right things at all times, in all circumstances, public or private.

Others are paying attention. They notice the company you keep. So hang out with honest people! Someone who is dishonest in little things will be dishonest in big things. If they can do it FOR you, they will do it TO you. This reminds me of a saying I used to hear as a child: "If you lie down with dogs, you will get up with fleas." You must always be seen as honest and trustworthy. Never allow yourself to do anything that might damage your integrity, or keep company with those who will reflect badly on it. Integrity takes a lifetime to build, but only a moment to lose. Let people doubt others--your word should be your bond. Allow for transparency. Protect your integrity. Put it all on the table.

Honesty: I have had the privilege of traveling around the world as a youth speaker. At one point, I received a call to do a series of workshops on a subject for which I did not feel qualified. However, I'd never been to this part of the world, and I wanted to go. The right thing to do would be to set aside my desires, and tell the people that this was not my area of expertise. Grudgingly, I made the call, and recommended someone who I felt was more qualified. To my surprise, the leaders insisted that they wanted me to come. I was excited, but more importantly, my integrity was intact, my conscience clean.

If I had not been totally aboveboard and honest with them, do you really think I would have gotten away with it? I doubt it. What if I got there and froze up because I was not ready to present the material? People want to believe in their leaders. As a leader, I must be trustworthy. When others know they can trust me, they're more likely to give me the benefit of the doubt. They'll be just as perceptive about my positive qualities as they are about the negative ones. It pays to practice honesty.

Modeling Ethics: As a society, we should be concerned about the ethics we are modeling. Kids are witnessing too much of the daily rip-off news. Successful people make it to the top of their game, but discover it's not enough. Leaders think they have everything arranged so that no one will find out, just to discover that they're only fooling themselves.

Positioning your integrity means you will always try to do the right thing. Surround yourself with values that foster contentment. A spirit of greed does not know how to be honest, ethical or moral; it's only about what I can get without being caught. I trust and pray that your desire to be used by God will keep you from falling prey to this perspective, so young people will have even more role models who illustrate the worth of integrity.

Accuracy: Live with the thought that everything must add up. Don't settle for the "penny off" mentality. I admire my daughter Raquel who is a CPA, though I have to admit that she used to drive me crazy with her need for accuracy. Everything had to be exact. She has contributed **immensely** to her father's maturity in the area of being accurate. She tells me "Dad, if one thing does not balance, then the whole thing is off." Because of her penchant for accuracy, Raquel's credibility is very high. I trust her to do the right thing with my taxes and retirement plan. No worries, though--if the retirement things doesn't work, out Maxine and I will just move in with Raquel and her husband!

Several popular American shows are all about settling legal disputes on national TV. Two of my favorites are *Judge Judy* and *Judge Joe Brown.* Judge Joe Brown challenges guys to "Man up!" And I am particularity impressed with Judge Judy's attention to detail. If she suspects you are not being truthful, it's over. There is little you can do to change her opinion of you. Your best bet is always to take a position of integrity from the start by telling the truth even if you are guilty. Say what you mean and mean what you say. And if you are repeating what someone else has said, know your source well or keep quiet. Certainly we all make mistakes; but being as accurate as possible will seriously increase the significance of your influence NOW.

Accountability: Seek out accountability, even if it's not required. Some people do not want to be held accountable because they feel it will limit them. Others are not going to function without it. Accountability, though uncomfortable at times, will provide safe parameters for getting to the next level of responsibility. Many years ago, I worked as a cashier in a grocery store. At the end of each shift we each had to close out our register. One night we had to work late. The interim manager was in a hurry to get to an appointment; he told all the cashiers that he would place their trays in the safe and someone would count them the next day. This was unprofessional and out of protocol, so none of the cashiers agreed to it. He had to miss his appointment because we took time to count the monies and make certain that everything added up before we left.

Positioning your integrity means you will make yourself accountable, and accept nothing less. If accountability is not practiced consistently, the temptation to indulge in questionable practices may overcome you. Every potential leader needs to surround themselves with individuals who will hold them accountable. Whether you are in business or in rehab, it is for your protection to always have someone looking over your shoulder. Choose at least one friend to help you in this manner. We all need people in our lives who know and love us, who will be bold enough to shine a light on the areas that need improvement, be they personal or professional.

From time to time, I host major conventions with thousands of youth and young adults. At the end of each one, participants are asked to complete an online evaluation. I also plan a staff debriefing session before we leave town. I appreciate the honesty and candor when someone points out a problem. Opening ourselves up to criticism not only fosters accountability, but also provides something to work on for next time. Accountability builds credibility and will increase the significance of your influence in God's plan.

Let's look at Ephesians 4:1-3:

> *In light of all this, here's what I want you to do. While I'm locked up here, a prisoner for the Master, I want you to get out there and walk—better yet, run!—on the road God called you to travel. I don't want any of you sitting around on your hands. I don't want anyone strolling off, down some path that goes nowhere. And mark that you do this with humility and discipline—not in fits and starts, but steadily, pouring yourselves out for each other in acts of love,* ***alert at noticing differences and quick at mending fences.*** (The Message)

Position Your Networking: None of us can handle God's plan by ourselves. Position yourself close to others who will help you meet that goal, climb that mountain. From what investors tell me, trying to corner the market by yourself or buying up your own stock is rarely a good plan for financial success. Diversifying is key; mix it up. The task God has prepared for you is bigger than any one person. You cannot do it by yourself; welcome others in the plan.

When a country faces the possibility of war, it seems that we always hear about its allies, no matter how great its military strength. Each nation wants others to stand with them, to bring their strength, resources and political clout to the table. Imagine the cost of war if it were not shared. A real ally is a true partner who is willing to take risks in an effort to keep the peace (or end hostilities). Being in the right position means having a group of people you can depend on. This is the essence of networking. You are "IT" in God's plan; who's helping you?

Positioning your network also means that the sharing goes both ways. Get plugged in to as many different networks as you can. Although ministry has been my focus for the last 30-plus years, I take pride in connecting with people in other areas of interest. I choose to attend conferences outside my primary field for the purpose of networking and exposure. I use my hobbies to increase my networks, as well growing my profession. When possible, I attend car shows, dog shows, boats shows, book reviews, motorcycle rallies, community rallies, inter-denominational functions, or DIY workshops. At these events, I meet lots of new people outside of my existing networks. Before you know it, we are exchanging business cards and planning to get together for lunch.

Business cards and social networking are important tools. I had to learn the hard way about business cards. I just kept forgetting to keep some on me! If people do not have your contact information, they cannot follow up with you. You won't be taken seriously as a person of influence in God's plan. If no one knows how to contact you, your influence is limited.

Start today by growing your network, then position yourself for what God will do through you. Many people will want to connect with you in the God's exciting plan.

Position Your Work Ethic: What's your personal philosophy about work? If you are a hard worker, somebody is going to notice. People will want you on their team. Consider the illustration of reality TV; shows like "Survivor" demonstrate the contrasting consequences of mediocrity and whole-hearted effort. Some folks take opportunity for granted, while others realize that they are granted opportunities. We've all known people who are the first to arrive and last to leave. Be that person who takes pride in what they do; establishing a serious work ethic will always provide you a net gain.

Between 1901 and 2011, the Nobel Prizes and the Prize in Economic Sciences were awarded 549 times--to individuals who understood the importance of hard work, commitment and dedication. My father helped develop my work ethic when he made me rake the yard over and over until all the leaves were gone. (You can read about this in my book, *God's Got a Plan and I'm in It!* The chapter is called "Leave No Leaves Behind.")

Avoid the Rush Job: Give yourself plenty of time to do a job right. Rushing is never a good practice. Besides the fact that it can be stressful, you are likely to miss something when you're in a hurry. I learned this when painting a room in my house. I only had a short time to do it, and it showed. I had to do the job all over again. Do it right the first time: have a plan, organize, make sure you understand the task, then go to work. Work smart, but avoid unnecessary shortcuts. Take pride in what you do. When someone asks who did that, you won't have to be ashamed.

Follow Up: You are not finished until you check and re-check your work. Step away, then come back and look it over again. A good plumber will always check for leaks; it's amazing how much a leak can cost later. Be your own supervisor and position your work ethic as you prepare for God's plan. People of influence don't trust just anyone to report for them. Every painting I have has the artist's signature at the bottom. I would venture to say that the signature was the last thing placed on the canvas once the work was completed.

Increasing the significance of your influence now will take hard work, but the rewards are great. Plus, God expects no less from you. The tasks ahead are no joke, they're the real thing. Get ready because God has a plan and you're "IT"!

Position your Determination: Being "IT" in God's plan will not be easy. You will meet people who will refuse to join you, and some who will not accept your help. Even at your best, some may reject you. That's because they have never met anyone like you. Establish a determined reputation. Determination can make all the difference in the world.

Most of my life, I was told what I could not do. Even when I became a national youth ministry leader, I kept hearing what could not be done. That doubt and negativity became fuel for my determination. In my earlier years, I was not particularly good at convincing people that I could accomplish a particular task. But I knew that if I stuck with it, I would be successful. Those who doubted were always surprised when the goals were reached.

Some people will not care that you are preparing for God's plan--they may just want to take advantage of you. Don't be easy prey for anybody. Show some respect for yourself; stand up for what you believe. As the saying goes, "if you stand for nothing, you will fall for anything." Be intentional and deliberate in your determination.

What would have happened if David had backed down from Goliath? Or Joseph had been untrustworthy in Egypt? What if the blind man at the Pool of Bethesda had not called out to Jesus? What would've happened if the bleeding woman hadn't touched the hem of Jesus' garment? Or a desperate father had not brought his son to be healed? What if the paralytic's friends had given up on getting him inside to see Jesus? We don't have to answer those questions, because their determined actions placed them in history. Their influence increased significantly because of their determination

I get frustrated when I see people of influence fail to stand up for what is right. Injustices take place right in front of their eyes, and they turn their heads. Some say, "It's not my problem," or "I can't do anything about it anyway." Don't give up without a fight when someone has been wronged. You may be their only hope. If you don't help them, who will? These are legitimate fights. I don't like to fight, but I will if I have to. I fight for what I believe, for righteousness. I fight for justice; I fight for the good of others.

God will use you to change things, so hold onto your determination. When you are determined, you are positioned to increase the significance of your influence. God wants to work with you as you prepare to be used in His plan.

God's Got a Plan and YoU're It!!!

Increasing the significance of your influence NOW

Chapter Five

My PRAYER:

Dear God,

I need Your help to position my availability, my integrity, my networking, my work ethic, and my determination NOW. Please give me the guidance I need to know your will.

My PLAN:

From this day forward I will…

1.

2.

3.

4.

5.

6.

7.

Signature____
Date_________________________

CHAPTER 6
PARTICIPATE WITH OTHERS IN THE PLAN

we saw others casting out demons...

Although I am challenging you to be "IT" in God's plan, you are not the only tool God has.

In Luke 9:49-50, Jesus' disciples thought they were the only ones using the power of Jesus to heal and cast out demons. They were shocked when they saw others with the same mission, doing the same things they were doing. They were ready to start a "holy war." But Jesus made an important statement: "Those who are not against us are with us." You may not know them all by name, but they're out there. The Twelve were surprised to find that they were not the only ones. Remember, God does not have to use us--He chooses to use us.

Participate by way of Inclusion: Learn to look beyond yourself from the start. You are not expert or experienced in everything. An attorney friend of mine took a case representing a client who was injured on a charter fishing trip. When the case came to trial, he realized that there was a weakness in his argument: he had never talked to the charter company to find out about licensing procedures and safety regulations (which included passenger compliance). Failure to include that knowledge cost him a case he should have won. Yes, he is my friend--but not my attorney.

Participating via inclusion means getting everyone involved in the plan. From the least to the greatest, everyone has something to offer. Oftentimes everyone but you can see this. There's a fine line between stubbornness and determination! It bothers me to hear someone say, "I've got this," when it is obvious that the only thing they've "got" is a big mess on their hands.

Have you ever thought about intentionally including the "little guy"? The one no one respects or pays attention to? Several years ago, I attended a meeting at the downtown Marriott in Oshawa, Canada. I parked my rental car in the garage and did not come out until three days later. I didn't realize how extensive the parking area was until I was looking for my car to return to the airport. It had something like 6 levels with 5 colored sections each. You've got it--I could not remember for the life of me where I had parked my car! My flight was departing in 90 minutes so I searched frantically. As I walked across one level, a homeless fellow approached and asked if he could help. I figured he was only interested in money, so I brushed him off.

I enlisted the hotel bellmen and security guards to help, but to no avail. All of us ignored the homeless man, who was still hanging around. Frustrated and angry at missing my flight, I fumed at having to pay for another flight the next day, $115.00 for another night in the hotel, $50 a day for the car, plus another $15 a day for parking. You do the math.

Later that evening, I saw the homeless man again. He asked if I had found my car; I said no. Once again he offered, "Can I help you find your car?" Realizing I had nothing to lose at that point, I agreed. Before we started this new search, he asked me a series of questions. Was there anything unique about the space I parked in? I remembered it was a tight space next to a wall and some stairs. He immediately informed me that my car was definitely in one of six places--every level had a space like that in the blue section. Together we checked that location on each level. Sure enough, there was my car--on level three in the blue section.

I was mortified that I had failed to include this guy in my search. His participation could have saved me a lot of time, money, and irritation. In God's plan, be prepared to participate with the unexpected—and the "least of these." That homeless man's influence increased significantly in my mind because of his helpfulness and his specific knowledge. There's room for everyone in God's plan.

Participate by Acceptance: What is the standard for acceptance? Ask this question and you'll get a different answer each time. Accepting someone's participation does not mean you have to agree with them on everything. Nor does it mean that you're endorsing everything they believe. Learn to meet people where they are, to value those who differ from you in standards, values, beliefs, religion, etc.

A few years ago, I was working with a youth community project in Dallas. A kid who was gay wanted to participate. Some folks had a problem with it, but I just saw a young person who wanted to help get the job done. As a Bible-believing Christian, I do not endorse homosexuality, but neither do I discriminate against homosexuals. I believe Jesus would take the same position. (Luke 15:1-2)

If you are in God's plan, all kinds of people should feel safe around you. You should have everybody's back. Imagine how embarrassed you might feel if a person you rejected turns up in another context as part of your Christian family. Now you have to act like everything is ok! Awkward…

Search and rescue teams don't necessarily share the same values or beliefs. But they do share a common goal: RESCUE. How would it sound if the ambulance crew asked what church you belonged to before they'd splint your broken leg? Or if the paramedics refused to treat someone of a different gender or skin color? You'd think they had lost their minds. If I am drowning, I don't care about the lifeguard's religion, race, or sexual orientation, whether they prefer paper or plastic. Just SAVE ME already!!! Do not expect people to change before you'll accept their participation in God's plan. After all, it IS God's plan, not yours. Accepting those He sends to participate with you can only increase your influence for His cause. God's got a plan and you're "IT"!

Participate with Solutions: There are two types of people in the world: those who love to talk about the problem, and those who want to find solutions. Participating in the solution means avoiding arguments and lengthy discussions. From my observation, most people seem to spend more time talking about problems than solving them.

Early on in my ministry, I conducted workshops dealing with critical concerns about our youth. People would tell me that they enjoyed the workshops, so I thought I was good at it--until I read one particular evaluation. The person said, "You are an expert at talking about the problem, but you provide few solutions." Ouch!!!! Though my professional ego was a little offended, I reviewed my outline, and sure enough, they were right. Discovering that truth was one of the best things that ever happened to me. Yes, I had a burden on my heart and I wanted to bring awareness, but if I did not participate in the solution, the problems would continue.

Once you get everyone together at the table, finding solutions can be pretty simple. Start by trying to understand the problem; see if you can determine how it began and what factors are contributing to it. The Band-aid approach is just that, a cover-up. However, applying the ointment of resolution provides healing. The answers are all around you; just let them through. Every situation has one or more solutions, whether the problem involves your personal life, finances, school, friendships, courtships, marriage. Applying the solution may not be entirely pleasant, or bring instant relief. But let it work for a while and it will change your circumstances.

Make certain you are participating with solutions. Brainstorm some answers instead of questioning everything. Be the plan, be the information "go-to" person in your network. God's got a plan and you're "IT"!

Participate by Involvement: Don't tell me how to plow--plow with me. Don't tell me how to plant--plant with me. People are more likely to follow you if are involved with them. Don't be afraid to lead by getting your hands dirty.

Following my studies at Andrews University Theological Seminary in Berrien Springs, Michigan, I was assigned to two churches in Lubbock and Amarillo, Texas. I was excited about my first district. Surely I would impress them with my theological jargon! Upon my arrival in Lubbock, I discovered that impressing the members with post-graduate education would have to wait. The roof of the church was about to cave in. The view from the pulpit was unbearable.

It was obvious that there was wind and storm damage, so we filed an insurance claim. Within days, the insurance adjuster was on the scene. We got the check, and I figured that we could do the repair job ourselves. The men of the church thought I was joking, until we organized everything and set a date. Everyone came out to help. We stripped off the old shingles and installed a completely new roof to match the recently painted church.

We saved hundreds of dollars because I was the first one on the roof, and the last one off. Sure, I was the pastor and ultimately responsible, but involving the men of the church in participation took us all to another level. I enjoyed four wonderful years in West Texas because involvement with people was a priority.

Participating in involvement means asking for an assignment no one else wants. It means recognizing that politics and titles don't matter when it comes to helping people. It means being the first to arrive and the last to leave. After all, you're "IT" in God's plan, and it wouldn't do to be late!

Participate with Strategy: Talk is cheap. So you plan to conquer the world for God--but you have no plan, no strategy, no idea where to start. This world is evil and the enemy is proud. Don't think for a second that he is going to let you waltz in and take over, just because you say you are in God's plan.

Participating in God's plan with strategy means always having a plan, even if it's a simple one. Sketch out how you hope to get from point A to point B. I have discovered that table napkins are an excellent medium for laying out such a strategy. Picture your ink pen rolling over the barbeque sauce you just wiped from your face! When the idea comes, don't wait--write it down.

Lone Star Camp in Athens, Texas was one of my many responsibilities as newly elected conference youth director. Several people brought me their ideas on a daily basis. Vernon Taylor, a native of East Texas, is a natural-born cowboy who understands everything about horses. We needed to resurrect the horsemanship program and be able to sustain it. Vernon said he had a strategy. I told him to write it down and bring it back to me. Like a typical cowboy, he went to the cafeteria, got a napkin and laid out the plan right there. I was impressed. Within a few years, we developed one of the largest horsemanship programs in the country.

Good strategies must. . .

- Be clear
- Be workable
- Be believable
- Be detailed
- Take nothing for granted
- Be reviewed and analyzed periodically
- Have a destination

Participating with strategy will definitely increase the significance of your influence; this makes it easier for people to follow and respect your mission for God. You are "IT" in God's strategy, so participate!

God's Got a Plan and YoU're It!!!

Increasing the significance of your influence NOW

Chapter Six

My PRAYER:

Dear God,

I need Your help as I learn to participate with others by acceptance, with solutions, and with strategy. Please give me the guidance I need to know your will.

My PLAN:

From this day forward I will…

1.

2.

3.

4.

5.

6.

7.

Signature____

Date______________________________

CHAPTER 7
PRACTICE FOR THE PLAN

Putting Your Hand to the Plow...

Never take the plan for granted. You may think you're ready, but how often do you practice? Every sports team has to practice their game plan. Executing the perfect play requires practice. When I was young, I never understood why someone who completed a medical degree plus two years of residency would need to establish a "practice." My doctor friends tell me that medicine is a rather inexact science because of the complexity of the human body and its environment. When someone gets sick, doctors don't necessarily know what will work until they try different remedies. Hence a medical or dental "practice."

As God is preparing you to be "IT" in His plan, you need to practice good habits. Jesus said in Luke 9:62, "No man, putting his hands on the plow and looking back, is fit for the kingdom of heaven." Heaven is about looking forward. If you want to become really good at something, you practice. This applies to feeding homeless people, mentoring youth, addressing the needs in your community. If you want to be seen as the world's most caring person, then practice. Have you ever heard that "practice makes perfect"? A music teacher friend tells me instead that "practice makes permanent." We want those good habits to be here to stay!

Practice Asking

Jesus says in John 16:24, "Ask and you will receive, that your joy may be full." You'll never know what can happen in God's plan until you ask. Thousands of people have experienced changed lives just because they asked.

Growing up in a large family had its challenges. When my mother cooked, she had to have a plan in order to feed eleven of us. Many times, seconds were not possible--but we would ask anyway. Sometimes we would get more food; other times we would not. However, she would always say that we wouldn't get seconds unless we asked. It wasn't automatic and should not be taken for granted.

Asking informs. You will only get an answer if you ask the question. I still remember what my seventh grade teacher, Miss Henriques, told our class: the only dumb questions are the ones you don't ask. If you appreciate getting good information, you should not mind asking. Besides, asking repeatedly allows you to practice receiving as well!

Asking clarifies: Several years ago, I had to participate in a deposition with my attorney. I was asked a series of questions about an incident I had witnessed. The opposing attorney tried to make it appear that I didn't know what I was talking about. However, the questions my attorney asked clarified the matter, so there was no need for another round. Make certain you have asked all the right questions. You need clarity in order to proceed with the plan.

Asking proposes: Practicing asking puts the deal out there. In the business world, you place a proposal on the table to find out if a client wants to do business. In the world of courtship, once you propose, the answer is either "I do" or "I don't." If your proposal is not accepted, then ask someone else when the time is right. Seriously, just keep courting! Asking gets answers.

Practice Seeking

Seek and you shall find. (Matt. 7:7) Not everything in life is at our fingertips. Some of the better opportunities have to be actively sought out. Practice looking for what is important to you. One of my favorite Bible chapters is Luke 15, which tells of the search for the lost sheep, the lost coin, and the lost son. Each was valuable, and missed when lost. Each was actively sought and found.

Seeking creates awareness; perhaps you will find other valuables along the way. Seeking gets results. The more you search, the more you discover in God's plan. Do you know anyone who is lost? Are you searching for them? Remember, you are "IT."

Practice Knocking

Knocking gets attention. My grade school teacher used to knock on her desk to bring the class back to order. She never figured out that it was a short term solution, but it still got our attention. In God's plan, knocking suggests you are making noise for a purpose. Maybe you are knocking on behalf of a cause that might not survive otherwise. My son almost got me in trouble when he was child. He came in the house and reported that a neighbor had made an unkind remark. I went to the neighbor's house and knocked on the door several times before there was an answer. I tried my best to be an adult about the situation but it did not turn out that way. That knock did not work out.

Knocking announces that someone is trying to get your attention for a particular purpose. It could be a salesman, surveyor, a neighbor or visitor. You have to open the door to find out. And you'll never know who might answer the door if you don't knock. Knocking gets a response; people are conditioned to respond to a knock. "Who's there? May I help you?" Someone knocking at your door suggests that you are needed in God's plan. And God urges us to practice knocking on His door to ask for what we need.

Practice Persistence

Once is seldom enough. The breakthrough in God's plan may not come the first time around. As a pastor, I have tried to help many people over the years. Some situations are easier than others; sometimes your help is accepted, while other times it is not. The key is practicing persistence. It may take months or years before progress is realized, but being persistent pays off for the one in need.

I admire the man in Luke 11:5-8 who was persistent about getting help for his family. He wouldn't take "No" for an answer. Because knocked persistently, his friend actually got out of bed and served him. Opportunity and results will awaken in your life if you're persistent.

How often do you practice asking, seeking and knocking? When the answer is "No," you can come back later to try again. The door to salvation will eventually open in God's plan. Stand back and watch your influence increase as others notice the fact that you practice what you preach and believe. God has a plan and you're "IT."

God's Got a Plan and YoU're It!!!
Increasing the significance of your influence NOW

Chapter Seven

My PRAYER:

Dear God,

Help me to consistently practice asking, seeking, and knocking. Please give me the guidance I need to know your will.

My PLAN:

From this day forward I will…

1.

2.

3.

4.

5.

6.

7.

Signature____
Date________________________

CHAPTER 8
PROTECT THE PLAN
defender of the faith

People generally protect what is valuable to them. If you have a mortgage on your home, you must have insurance. No one can drive a new car off a dealer's lot without insurance. Insurance does not prevent accidents; it just provides some protection in case of one.

Jesus protected the woman caught in adultery. (John 8:1-11) The hypocrites were ready to stone her, but Jesus had a different plan. His plan was not about excusing her sin. Instead, He pointed out the hazards of jumping to conclusions. The accusers had sin in their lives too, and were protecting each other. Jesus rebuked their actions by writing out their sins. Once they had all slunk off, He said to the woman, "Go, and sin no more." Because of My forgiveness, you are now free. Forgive yourself and don't return to the lifestyle that entrapped you.

Forgiveness means to pardon, exonerate, let go; to forget about; to give another chance. Many people doubt their ability to move forward because of past guilt. Some things seem too awful to be forgiven. But God's forgiveness covers the past. He does not hold it against us. We are freed from the guilt of sin and its eternal consequences.

Perhaps you have accepted God's forgiveness of your sins, but still find it hard to forgive yourself. Don't let guilt reign in your life and bind you to your past. I can definitely remember those struggles. I gave my heart to God and thought everything was fine; then my conscience started playing games. I plodded along like this for several years, until I realized that God had forgiven me, so I might as well forgive myself!

God has a plan and you're in it. He wants you to experience His forgiveness--and to forgive yourself. Guilt and past challenges cannot come along with you on this special journey. Stop right now; exorcise those demons from your life and forgive yourself as God has forgiven you.

Pray this simple prayer:

> "Dear God, I confess my past sins and mistakes. I thank You for sending Jesus to die for my sins. Because of His sacrifice I accept your forgiveness. Please give me the strength now to forgive myself and be free of the past. I choose to move forward in Your name, knowing that I am totally forgiven. In Jesus' name, Amen."

On a personal note, I desperately needed God's help to forgive those responsible for my 17-year-old brother's death long ago. I also needed His help to forgive myself, because deep down, I felt that I should have been able to prevent it. Thankfully, God's power and forgiveness prevailed in my life. Though I still have my days, I don't live with anger, or the guilt that once gripped me. Truly, God will come through for you if you let Him.

The Bible teaches that everyone has an opportunity in God's plan. "I have come that they might have life, and that they might have it more abundantly." (John 10:10) The apostle Paul saw himself as both a beneficiary and defender of the faith. If you really value something, you will protect it. Do you value God's plan? Then protect it by standing up for it.

Protect the Weak

God is all about defending the defenseless. I have ministered in places where the poor had no voice--places like Haiti, India, and South America. I have seen homeless children on the streets with no sense of direction or hope. I've seen them nearly kill each other when a tourist gave one child a five dollar bill and told them to share it. That scene was unbelievable. In Mumbai, India, I saw many children begging on the streets with no protection other than their night-time hiding places. One elderly lady apparently functioned as a grandmother to dozens of street children. She too was homeless, but those children were her life. It was obvious to me that "her" children appreciated the significance of her influence. Who will protect those in poverty who have no voice of their own? Raise your voice with mine. Protect the weak in God's plan.

Every day, millions of children are abused worldwide. Let's look at the statistics:

- An estimated 1.2 million children are trafficked worldwide every year.
- An estimated 300 million children worldwide are subjected to violence, exploitation and abuse, including the worst forms of child labor in communities, schools and institutions.
- Children living in areas of extreme economic hardship and social disruption are at increased risk for abuse, violence, and exploitation.
- About 1.5 billion children lived in the 42 countries affected by violent conflict between 2002 and 2006. Of 14.2 million refuges worldwide, 41 percent may be children under the age of 18.
- Worldwide, an estimated 40 million children under the age of 15 suffer from violence, abuse and neglect.
- An estimated 1.2 million children–both boys and girls–are trafficked each year into exploitative work, including mining, factories, armed conflict or commercial sex work.

Sources: www.unicef.org, www.ispcan.org, www.ilo.org

Oftentimes, the abuse is taking place right in front of us. Many of them are terribly afraid and defenseless. Divorce, poverty, homelessness, and other evils lead to children being tossed around in systems that cannot always protect them. They are innocent; they are just children trying to get through this crazy world. Volunteer to be the "IT" for innocent children.

My mother, Claretha Black, is a hero to the dozens of children who passed through our Savannah, Georgia home in foster care. We have seen it all. However, I am grateful that two of my sisters, Patricia and Rosena, were influenced by our parents to continue providing quality foster homes for those who need protection.

Protect the Innocent

I was sitting in court once when the judge determined that someone had been falsely accused. Although the prosecutor had made a solid case, it was apparent that this man needed the court's protection, so the judge intervened. He also reprimanded the court-appointed defense attorney for not being prepared to help his client. If I am ever falsely accused, I do not want court-appointed help, but God-appointed help. I want someone who is God-appointed and God-anointed.

We must also reach out to the guilty. Think of those incarcerated. Society says they deserve punishment, but they are still human beings. Protect their rights for rehabilitation. Without the grace of God, any of us could have been where they are. Some are really hoping for a second chance. Maybe you can help find that opportunity for them. Why assume that everyone doing time is a habitual criminal? If we all make that assumption, they don't stand a chance when they are released. Volunteering for a Transitioning Program can be an excellent way to increase the significance of your influence NOW in God's plan.

The bottom line here is, always do the right thing without compromise. Use your influence for good, period. Being "IT" in God's plan means saying NO to partiality and discrimination. Jesus is our best example. He says, "I did not come to call the righteous, but sinners to repentance." (Luke 5:32) The significance of my influence is only because of his grace and mercy in my life. It can be the same in yours.

Protect the Faithful

Praise God for those who try to do the right thing! May you always be one of them, standing with those who honor God and determine to live for Him. Support the faithful few without compromise. Several years ago I was called to speak at a boarding academy in the southwest. I knew several of the students and their families quite well, and was looking forward to seeing them. However when I arrived, I was embarrassed to discover that those I knew were completely out of control and running amok.

A teacher pulled me aside in confidence and asked if I would address the issues with the principal. I agreed, and that discussion turned into a full faculty meeting. After listening to the concerns, I was convinced that the school had failed to implement appropriate disciplinary measures. When asked my opinion, I recommended that certain students needed to be expelled in order to regain the school's credibility and integrity. Needless to say, many parents blamed me for the actions taken against their kids. The faculty appreciated my support for this difficult decision. Several of the students who were expelled went on to get their act together and become very successful. Some continue to struggle. In hindsight, I am thankful that God gave me the peace of mind to protect and support those faithful educators.

In your journey, you may encounter some who need your support against the system. When God uses you to help build up His kingdom through your influence, He also expects you to stand up for those you have mentored and shepherded. It may not be popular standing alone, but for those you represent, it's worth every bit of courage. God's got a plan and you're "IT."

God's Got a Plan and YoU're It!!!
Increasing the significance of your influence NOW

Chapter Eight

My PRAYER:

Dear God,

Help me protect Your plan for the weak, the innocent, and the faithful. Please give me the guidance I need to know your will.

My PLAN:

From this day forward I will…

1.

2.

3.

4.

5.

6.

7.

Signature____________________________________
Date________________________

CHAPTER 9
PRESERVE YOURSELF IN THE PLAN

take my yoke...

Jesus says, "Take my yoke upon you... For my yoke is easy and my burden is light." (Matt. 11:29-30) The key is not just an easy yoke, but preservation with a light load. I have always been fascinated by communities that demonstrate exceptional longevity. One example is Loma Linda, California, which has been featured on several popular television shows. Seventh-day Adventist residents there live years longer than average because of a healthy and positive lifestyle. (For information about this health study, visit www.llu.edu.) God wants to you be around for a long time in His plan. Making the right decisions can increase your chances for quality and quantity of life.

Choosing a Career Path

Choosing the right long-term career can help you preserve yourself in God's plan. "What do you want to be when you grow up?" I remember how I used to hate that question. Sure, I could dream big and make up something, but I was not certain of anything--much less what I actually wanted to do. So I played the usual doctor-lawyer game, until I got to high school. Then I realized the classes that would prepare me for those career paths were not on my list. College offered another reality check: I became more convinced that whatever career path I chose would call for study, sacrifice and practice. Choosing a career path can be a frightening experience. Consider the following as you work on preserving yourself in God's plan:

1. What are my strengths and weaknesses?
2. What are my interests and what really drives me? (Identify occupations that match your interests.)
3. When I talk with someone in a field I'm interested in, does it resonate with me?
4. Can I operate my own business or work for someone else?
5. What things do I enjoy most?
6. What contribution will I make to society?
7. How might this impact my physical and mental well being?
8. Will this job allow me to maintain financial stability?
9. Can I do this long term?
10. If I'm already in a career, should I consider a change?

Choosing the right career path can bring joy, happiness and fulfillment to your life. Wouldn't it be awesome to have a job that didn't feel like work? Something you'd look forward to every day of your life? If you're a student, do you feel that way about your major field? Take time to talk to God about this, because your life may depend on it.

Many people are simply burned out, doing something that's "just a job" for 8-12 hours a day. You deserve to be happy with your life's work. If you're not on track for that, perhaps you need to consider a career change or make some adjustments. Your work should benefit your long-term well being.

I feel good about my work in youth and young adult ministry. Not only do I see God using me to impact lives, but I have so much fun doing it. I take it one day at a time; at the end of each day I want more! I appreciate the successes and the challenges, the highs and the lows of ministry. Recently, someone asked me how much longer I plan to continue in youth ministry. I responded, "Until I am not thinking about young people when I wake up in the morning." I don't ever want to do anything else. "Dear God, please preserve me in Your plan…"

Choosing a Life Partner

A life partner is just that--a partner for life. Loving and helping each other will help preserve you in God's plan. You should not take this choice lightly, since (hopefully) you will spend the rest of your life with this person. Given that you are going for the long-term, you want someone in your life who will be a blessing and complement God's plan.

Young people, enjoy life before you start obsessing about marriage. I see a lot of folks who think that they are in love after the first date. Dating too young can lead to early breakups. One day a couple is "going together," and the next day they are talking about "my ex." So by the time one has finished college or is prepared to think about settling down with a life partner, they may have a dozen "exes." Wow! Whatever happened to the good ol' days when friends were truly friends, and we just enjoyed each other's company until we knew what we wanted?

If you are single and looking, consider the following as you go about choosing a life partner:

1. Know when you're ready to look seriously
2. Know what you need and what you don't need
3. Understand the dating game
4. Ask the right questions at the beginning of the relationship
5. Look for someone who. . .
    - is spiritual
    - is compatible
    - shares your level of intellect

- will let you be yourself
- will bring out the best in you
- is secure
- is open-minded

Hopefully these ideas will help you get started. Begin praying now that God will introduce you to the person He has created just for you. Also, pray that God will prepare you for that person as well. The person you choose will help make or break you in the long-term plan God has prepared for you, so don't take them for granted.

If you are already committed in a marriage, rest assured that all of God's power is available to help you grow and improve that relationship. The biggest room in the world is the room for improvement. It is always a good idea to periodically re-evaluate your marriage and make certain that all aspects are working well. Marriage was meant to be a blessing and not a burden.

Preserve yourself by accepting help

When the opportunity presents itself, split the work with someone else and preserve your strength. While living in Dallas, Texas, I came upon a lady who was stranded on the highway with a flat tire. I pulled over and offered to assist her, feeling great about the chance to be of service. To my surprise, she cursed me out and told me where I could take my help--it was not to heaven! My little heart was broken. I went on to my appointment, and when I returned an hour and a half later, I saw that she was still struggling with her tire. But I was not about to test God's plan again.

Often I see young people rejected when they are trying to help or offering a contribution to the mission. I have never seen a one-man army.

Enjoy the view--let someone else drive every now and then. Catch up on your sleep and let someone else do that task. Burnout is not an option for you. This could be the time in your life where you start delegating more and realize how gifted you really are. You can only benefit from help if you accept it. Preserve yourself in the plan.

Preserve yourself by working smarter

You have heard the saying, "don't work harder--work smarter." Just because you sweat at a task does not mean you did it right. Working smarter may mean stepping back and reassessing, taking a good look at things to see if there is a more productive way.

One thing I appreciate about my son: he is definitely going to find the easiest way, the shortest route. Although we sometimes have clashed about this, I respect the fact that he takes a good look to see if there is a better way. Keep in mind that the shortest route may not be the best or the safest route. The same is true for the longest route. Take time to plan your journey; preservation and pace are the important in your mission plan for God.

Preserve yourself with a decent pace

I love the word "pace." It sounds so pleasant, so balanced and non-stressful. Your pace is something you establish; it is not necessarily determined by someone else. You get to set your own pace and stick to it. It can always be adjusted. If you wear out early in the game God cannot use you as effectively.

Backpacking can teach some valuable lessons about pace. Because of the load you carry, you must strategically plan your route and pace your way through it. A consistent pace allows you plan your time. Your feet may get blistered, you may sweat profusely, and the darkness of night will surely come. However, the load will lighten as you use up your supplies, and the end is in sight. Preserving your pace allows you to accomplish things you might have thought impossible.

Preserve yourself in the plan; God has a serious hike planned for you and your network.

Preserve yourself in the Plan because you are "IT"!

There is only one of you, and you're needed. It is humbling to think that God allows us to be "IT" in His plan. By God's grace, let's be the best we can for the good of mankind. Just like Christ came to be "IT" for our salvation, God can use us to make a difference in the lives of those around us. As the young people say, "don't get it twisted!" God does not need us; by His grace he chooses us to be "IT" in His plan. The humbling part about this is that there will always be someone better, but He chose you! Therefore preserve yourself; you cannot be replaced. God only created one of you and you are "IT."

God's Got a Plan and YoU're It!!!
Increasing the significance of your influence NOW

Chapter Nine

My PRAYER:

Dear God,

I need Your help to preserve myself in the plan with my life choices, by accepting help, working smarter, and pacing myself. Please give me the guidance I need to know your will.

My PLAN:

From this day forward I will…

1.

2.

3.

4.

5.

6.

7.

Signature____
Date_______________________

CHAPTER 10
Praise and Celebrate the Plan
my son who was lost is now found...

Have you ever imagined yourself inside the story of Luke chapter 15? After being criticized and hated for hanging out with sinners, Jesus shared three parables about the lost sheep, the lost coin and lost son. Although each one got lost in the plan, they were all eventually found. Being found was such a big deal that Jesus specifically included praise and celebration in each story. It is a privilege to rejoice because we are in His plan. And being lost does not always mean being hopeless.

The Search

The search says much about the shepherd. Obviously, he cared enough that he could not relax while of his sheep was missing. The worry, the "what-ifs"—these things prompted the shepherd to leave the rest of the flock to go and search for the one. The Bible says he searched until he found the one he was looking for. God's awesome plan includes searching for lost sheep until they are found.

The Finding

Nothing is more frustrating than losing something–and nothing is more satisfying than finding "IT." I remember getting lost as a child at the county fair in Savannah, Georgia. There were eleven of us, and Mother and Daddy had the entire Black family looking for me. It took a long time for them to locate me, because I did not know I was lost. You see, I had free tickets to go on every ride, so that's what I did. While the others were worried about me, I was having the time of my life. When all my tickets were gone, I went up to a police officer and told him I was lost. He became an instant hero for "finding" me.

When my family came to the police office, they did not know whether to hug me or kill me. As I recall, the hugs won 8 - 2. (Two of my sisters weren't buying it.) The joy of finding me overshadowed the need for discipline. Maybe you have loved ones who seem lost; it's hard to reach them because they are enjoying the pleasures of the world. They know they have drifted far from God, but they aren't quite ready to return. God's plan says to keep searching; soon they'll be found, and celebration is just around the corner.

The Return

God wants to teach you how to bring someone home. The shepherd found the sheep, picked it up, placed it on his shoulder and carried it home. There is no indication that the sheep was injured--yet the sheep was carried home. This indicates a gentle, loving approach. Just imagine what might go through the mind of the sheep while riding home on the shepherd's shoulder. There were no words of condemnation or rebuke, just a free ride home! Have you ever been carried home? I have. So many times in my Christian journey I have gotten off the path, yet I ended up being carried home. God will always find a way to bring home His loved ones. The sheep just has to cooperate with the ride--to stop fighting and enjoy the view.

Others may not appreciate the return of the sheep, but it does not matter. The shepherd places him safely back in the fold, then says, "Let's have a party and rejoice--my sheep is home again!" Someone might mutter that this is not the first time that dumb sheep has taken off, but it does not matter to the shepherd. He's busy getting the party ready.

The Party

Everybody is invited to the party. In each of the three parables, the "searcher" said to all those around them, "Come and rejoice with me, for that which was lost is found!" Usually when there is a party everyone wants to know the occasion. Imagine an invitation that says, "Lost-but-found Party"! You may never know exactly when to schedule the party, but if you're "IT" in God's plan, you're always planning. I love "Lost-but-found" parties. They are different from all others.

One day, "soon and very soon," there is going to be an awesome party for the redeemed--for all those who were lost until the blood of Jesus found them. God is preparing you to serve every guest. The party starts here and ends in the kingdom of Heaven, then we start all over again. Just think--a party for eternity! The practice celebration begins now. The search is on. Thank you for being "IT" in God's plan.

God's Got a Plan and YoU're It!!!

Increasing the significance of your influence NOW

Chapter Ten

My PRAYER:

Dear God,

Help me praise and celebrate the plan by searching, finding, and returning Your lost ones, and by preparing for the party. Please give me the guidance I need to know your will.

My PLAN:

From this day forward I will…

1.

2.

3.

4.

5.

6.

7.

Signature____
Date________________________________

CONCLUSION

Hundreds of people have asked why I wrote the book, *God's Got a Plan and I'm In It!* The truth is, I woke up one morning, looked at my life, shook my head and realized that God has truly been gracious to me. Despite all my trials, tribulations, mistakes, lessons, heartaches, failures, a bunch of crazy stuff and many successes, God had me in His plan all along. As I reflect back, I wish someone had helped me realized it more. Now, because I am convinced I am in His plan, I run the race that is set before me with patience. (Heb. 12:1) I also keep in mind that in God's plan, everyone who endures to the end is a winner.

God knows everything about you. Regardless of how you view yourself, He sees you as an irresistible opportunity.

Maybe you feel it is not your business to engage in other people's lives. Please avoid this mentality. It IS your business, and you are open for business. What church needs more UN-caring people? You can make a difference by caring for others, because God has a plan and you're "IT" through Christ.

Finally, think of all the people God has used through the years to draw you closer to Him and to keep you faithful in His plan. Have you thanked Him for those faithful people, and for His plan? Be like the leper who returned. He could not resist; he had to say thank you for what was not deserved. God's grace and mercy is a gift, and it's all part of His plan for you.

God does not need us in His plan, but He allows us to participate for His glory. I'm certainly glad he does!

God's Got a Plan and YoU're It!!!
Increasing the significance of your influence NOW

My OPENING PRAYER:

Dear God,

Thank you for showing me how to increase my influence in your plan NOW. I am humbled and honored to be a part of your plan in making a significant difference in the lives of those around me and beyond. Please keep me faithful, focused, firm, fearless, and determined in your will for my life NOW as I commit myself to you eternally.

My COMMITMENT:

From this day forward, I choose to have a significant influence in God's Plan NOW

Signature ____

Date ______________________